Head over Heels

By Peter Contre

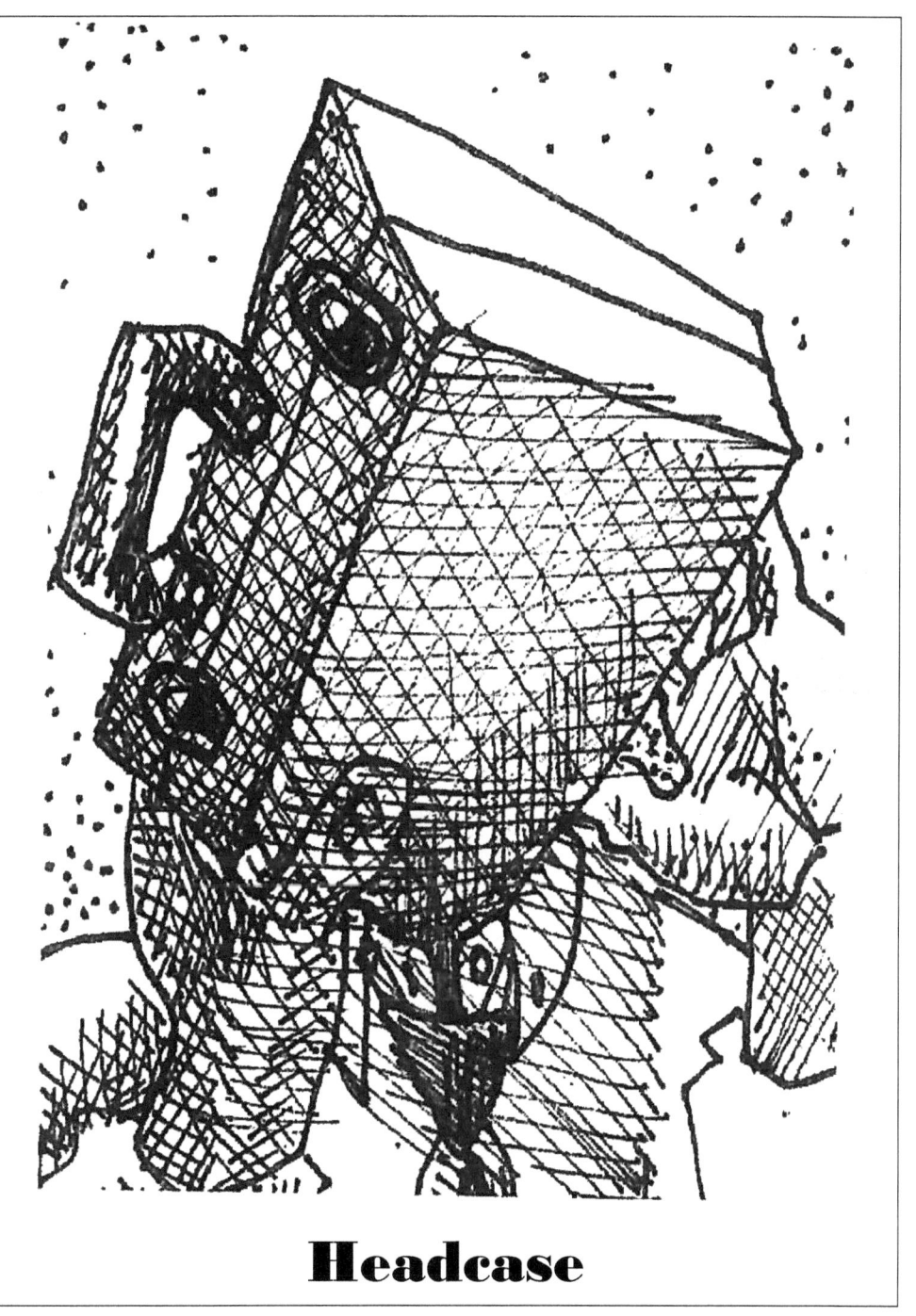

Headcase

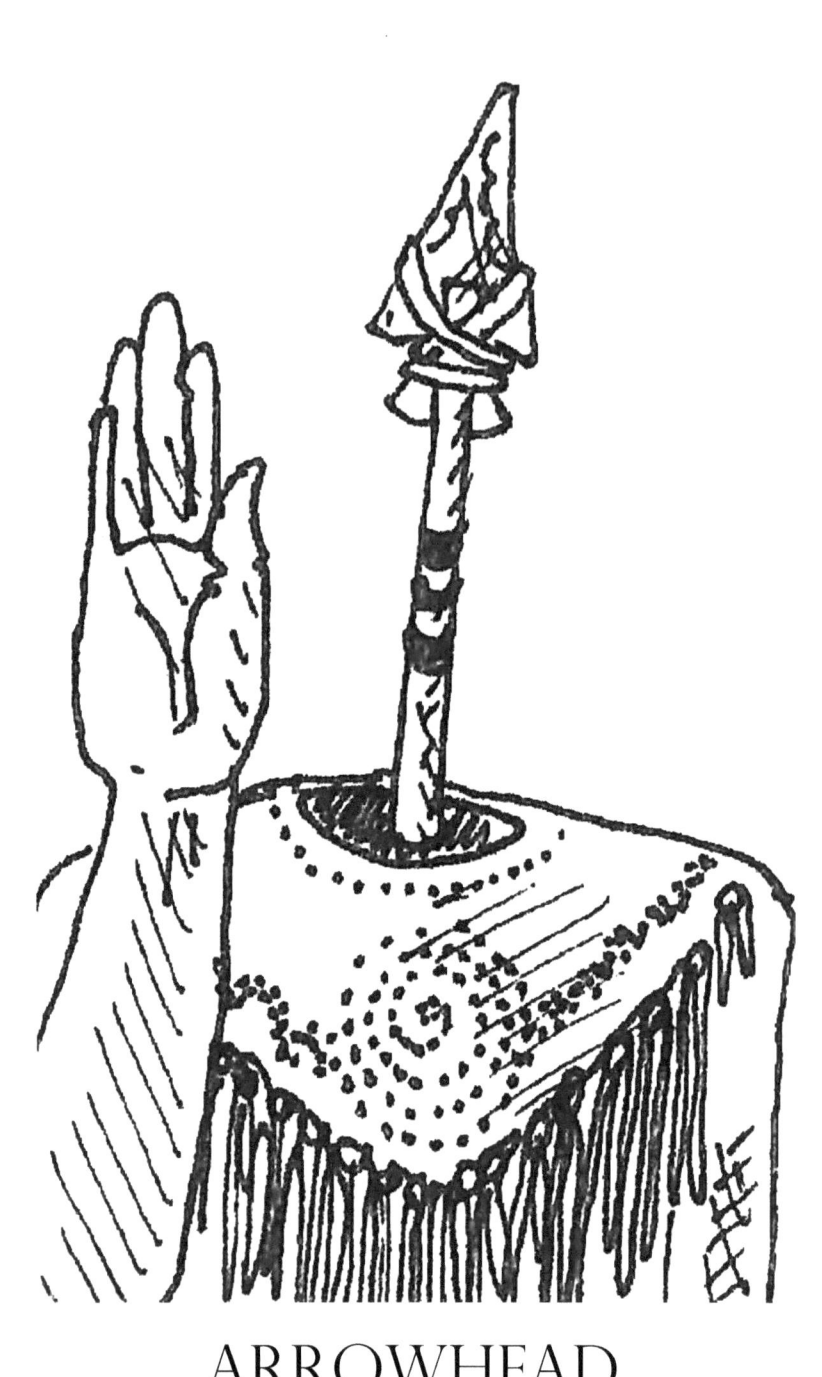

ARROWHEAD

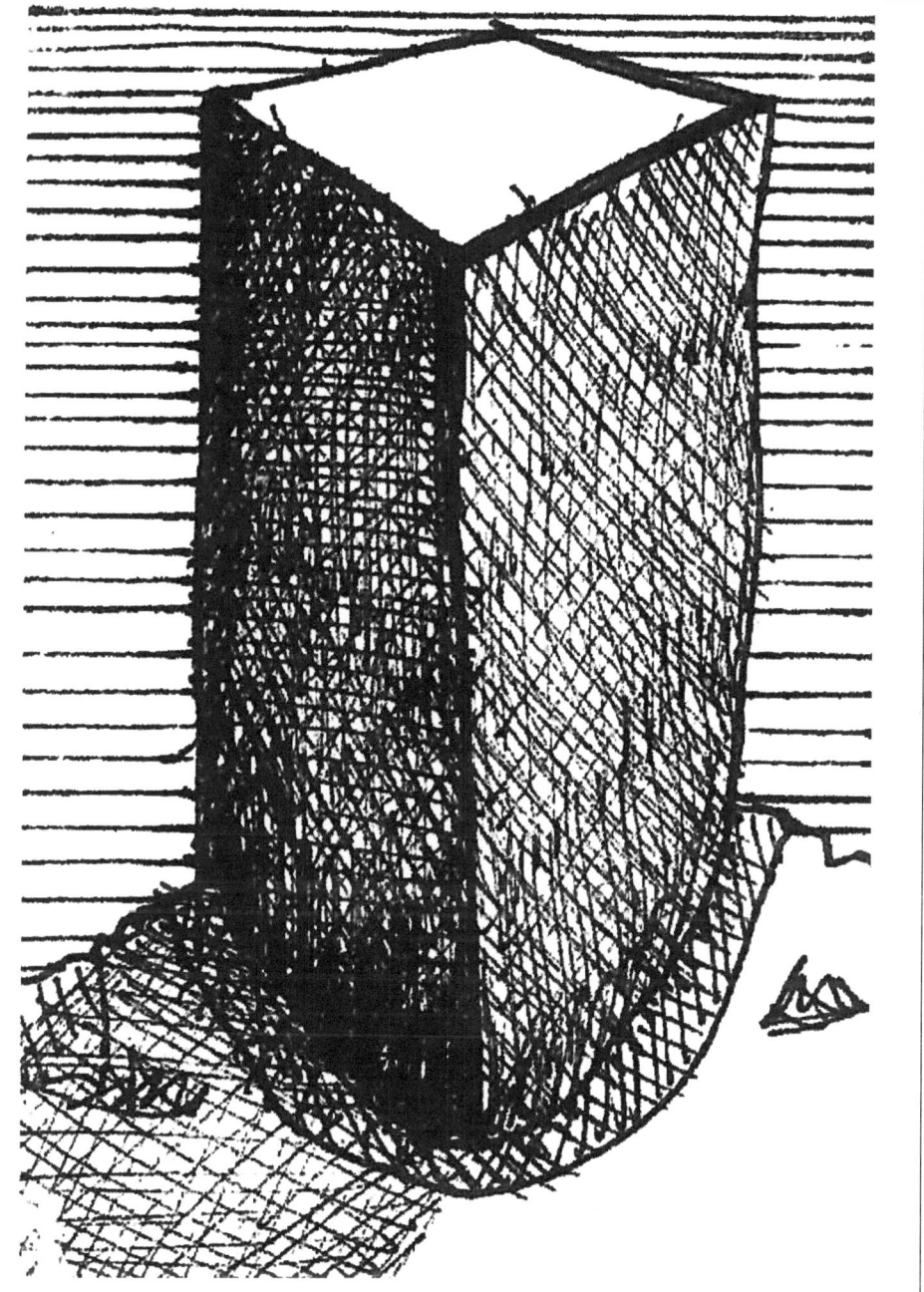

BLOCKHEAD

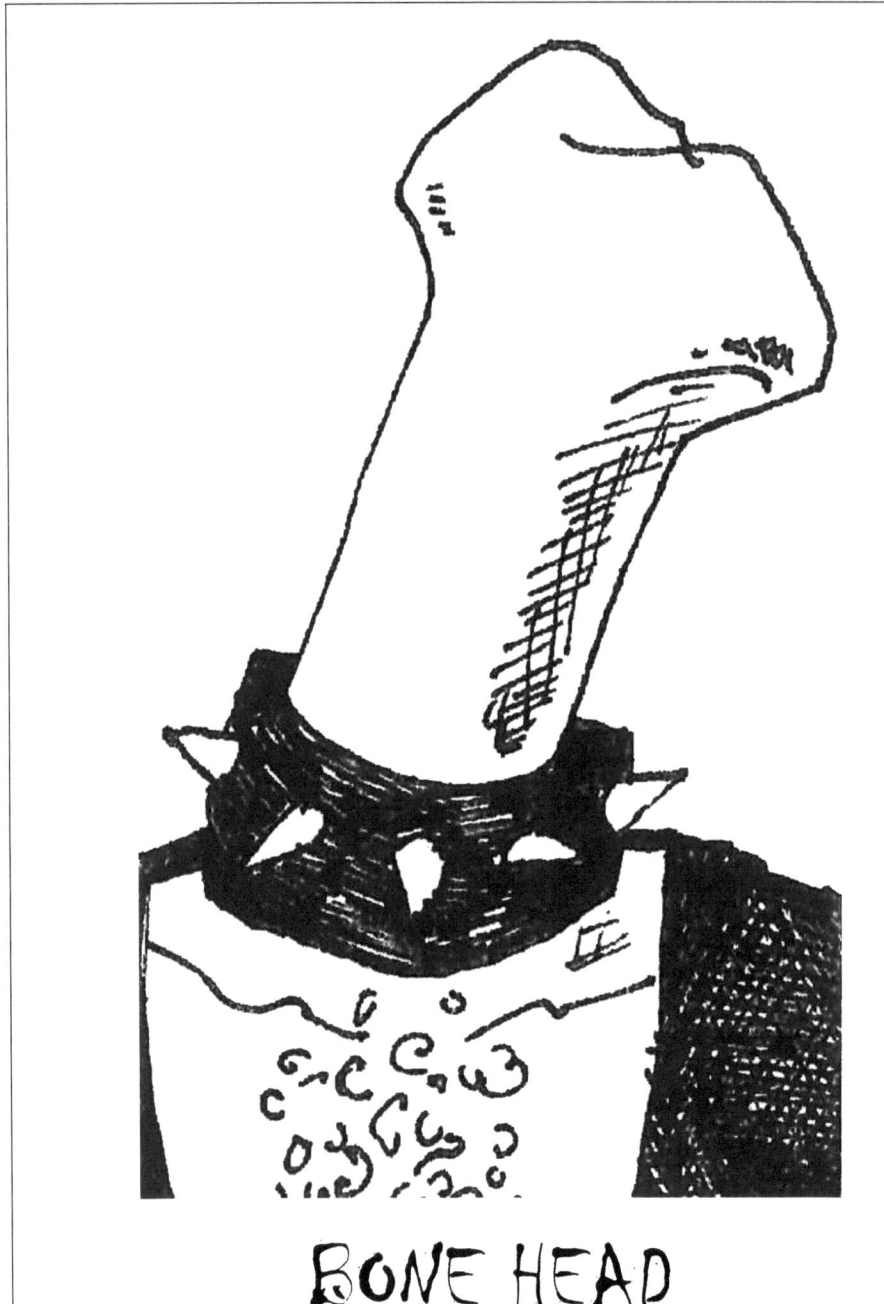

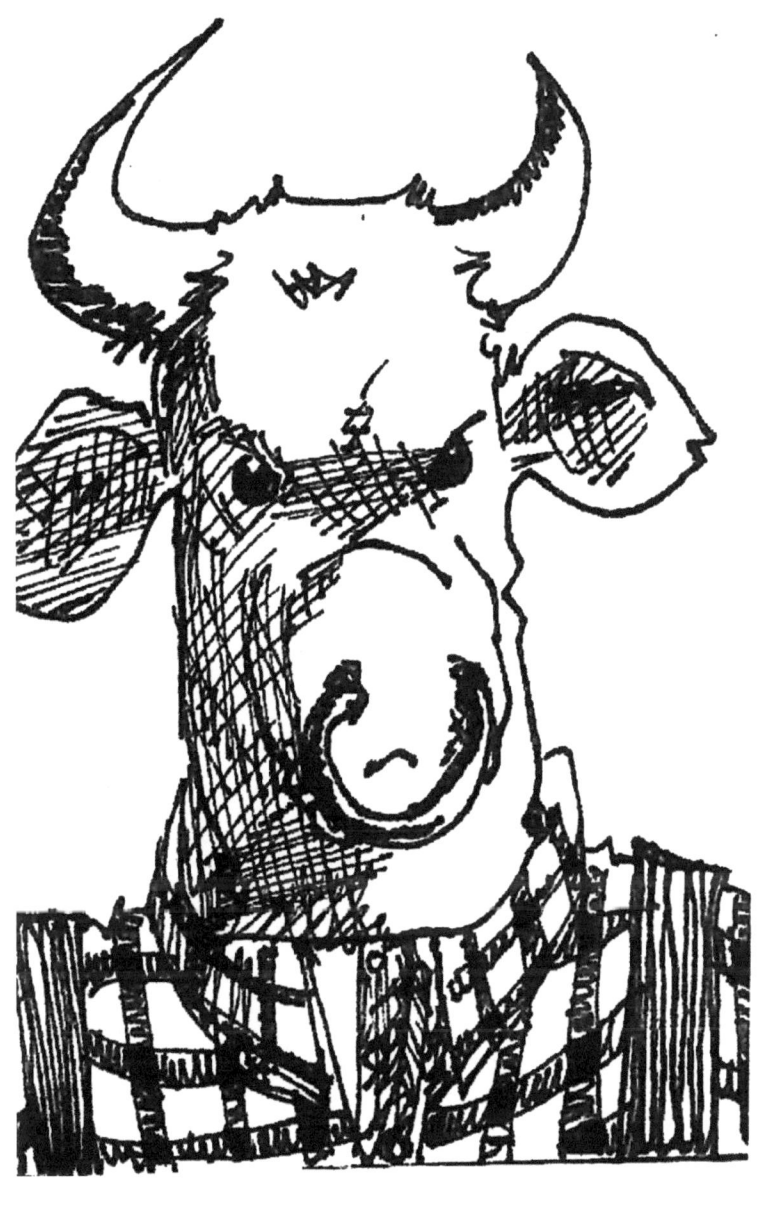

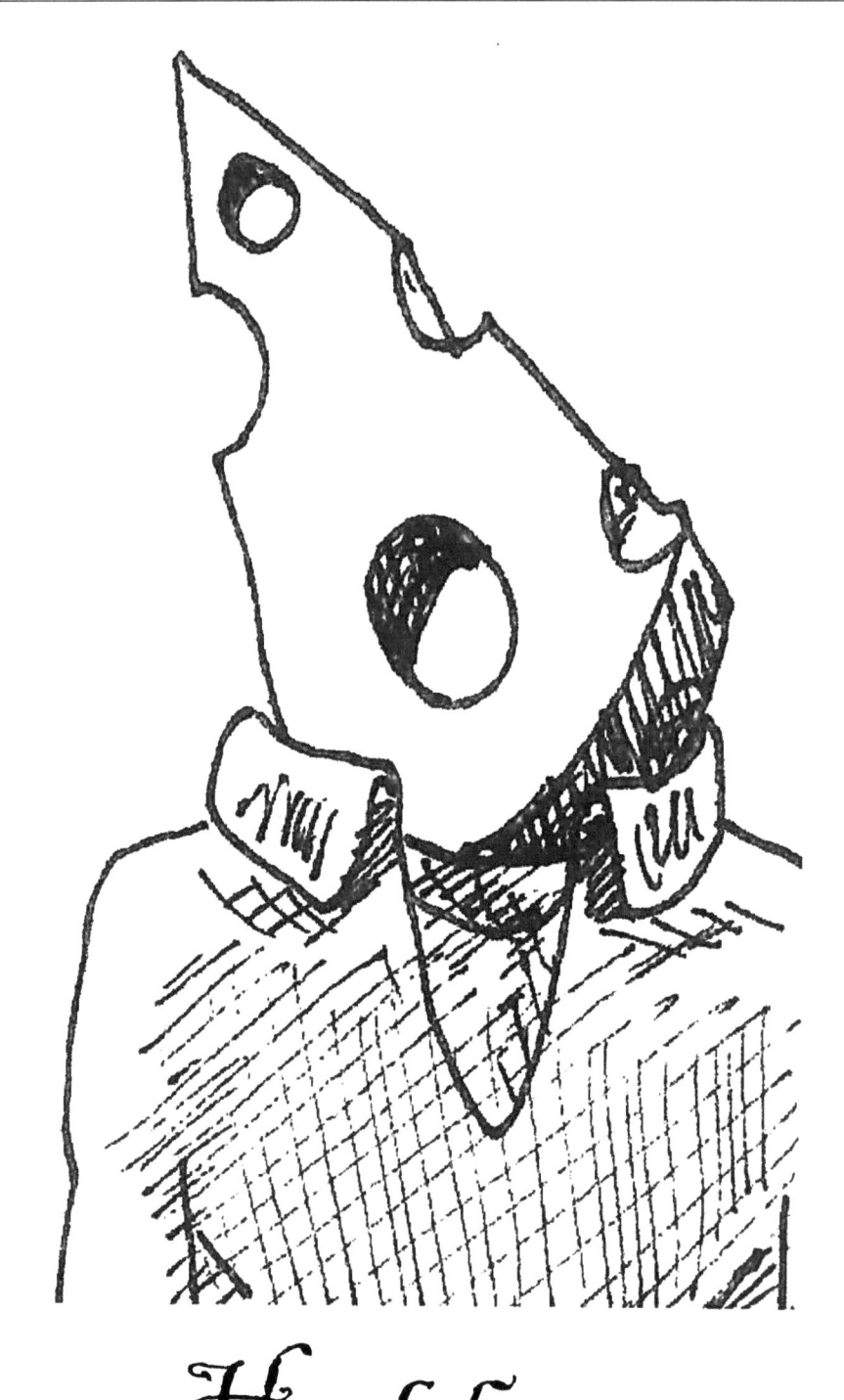

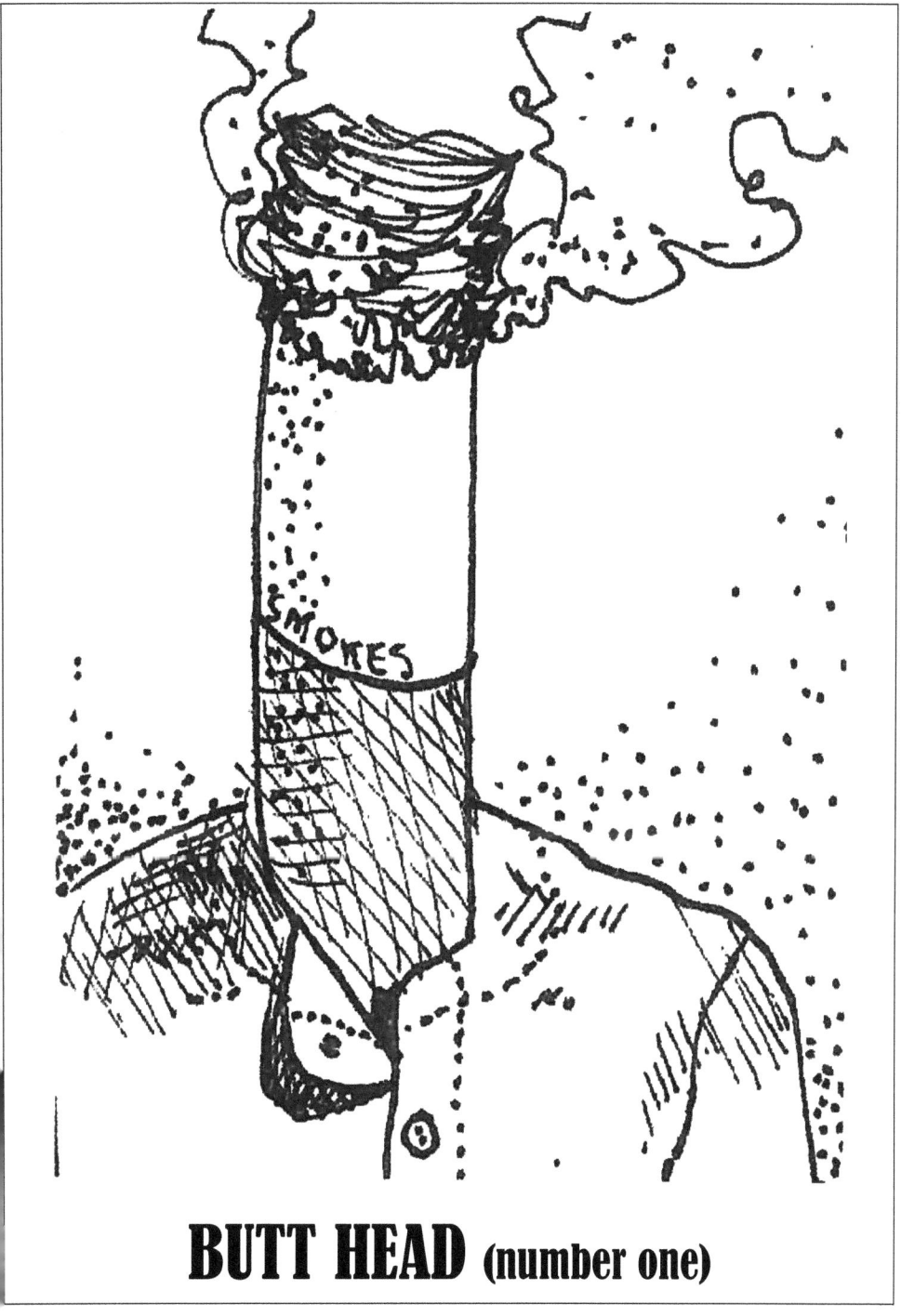

BUTT HEAD (number one)

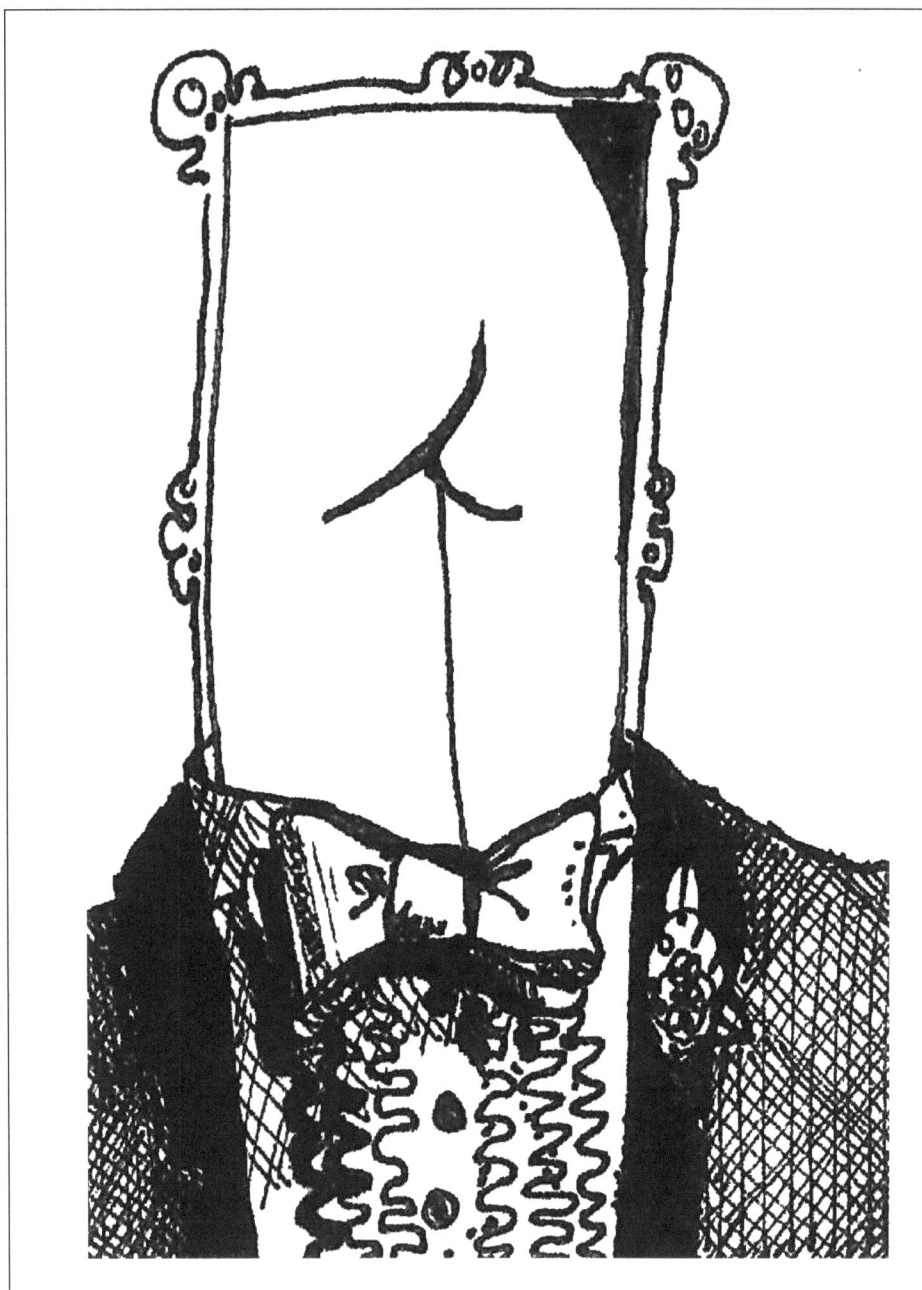

BUTT HEAD (NUMBER TWO)

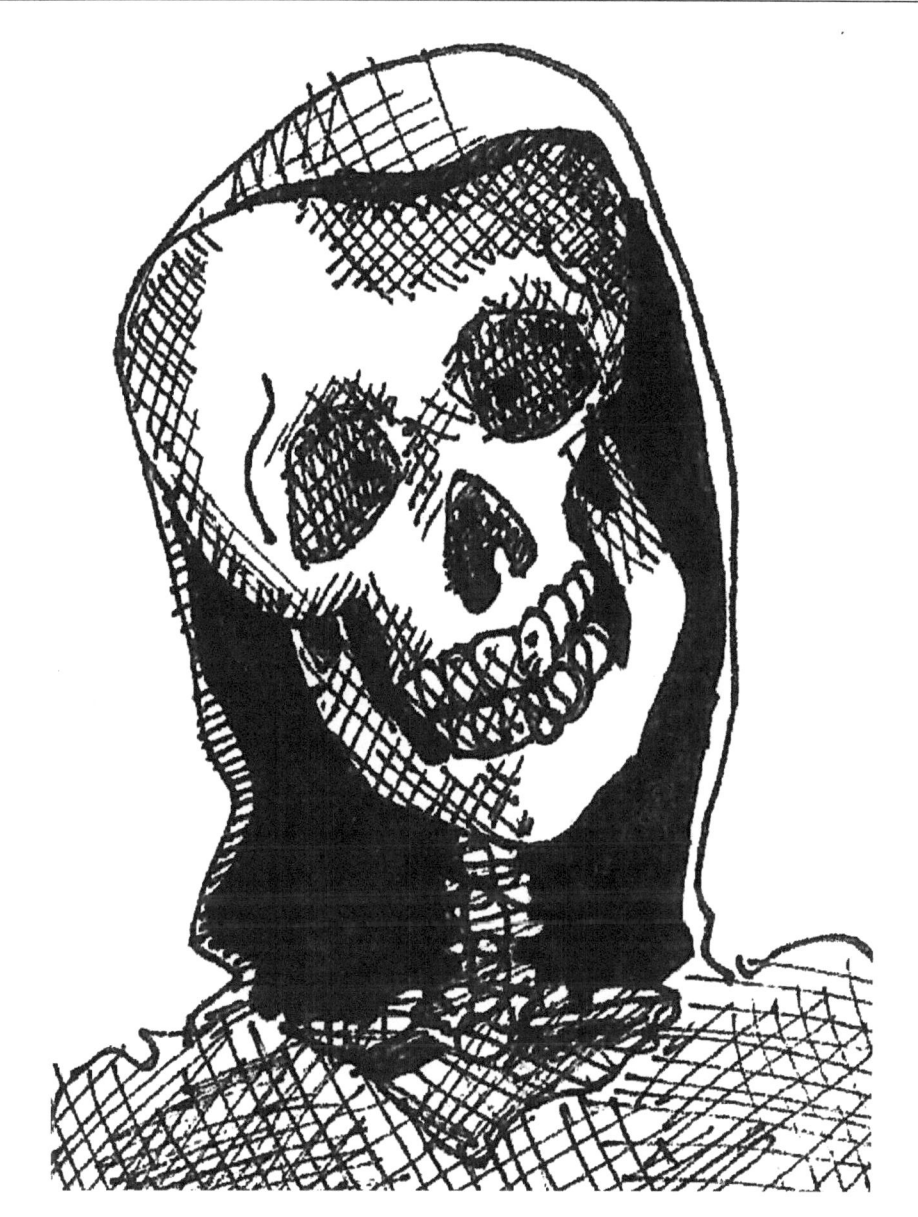

Dead Head

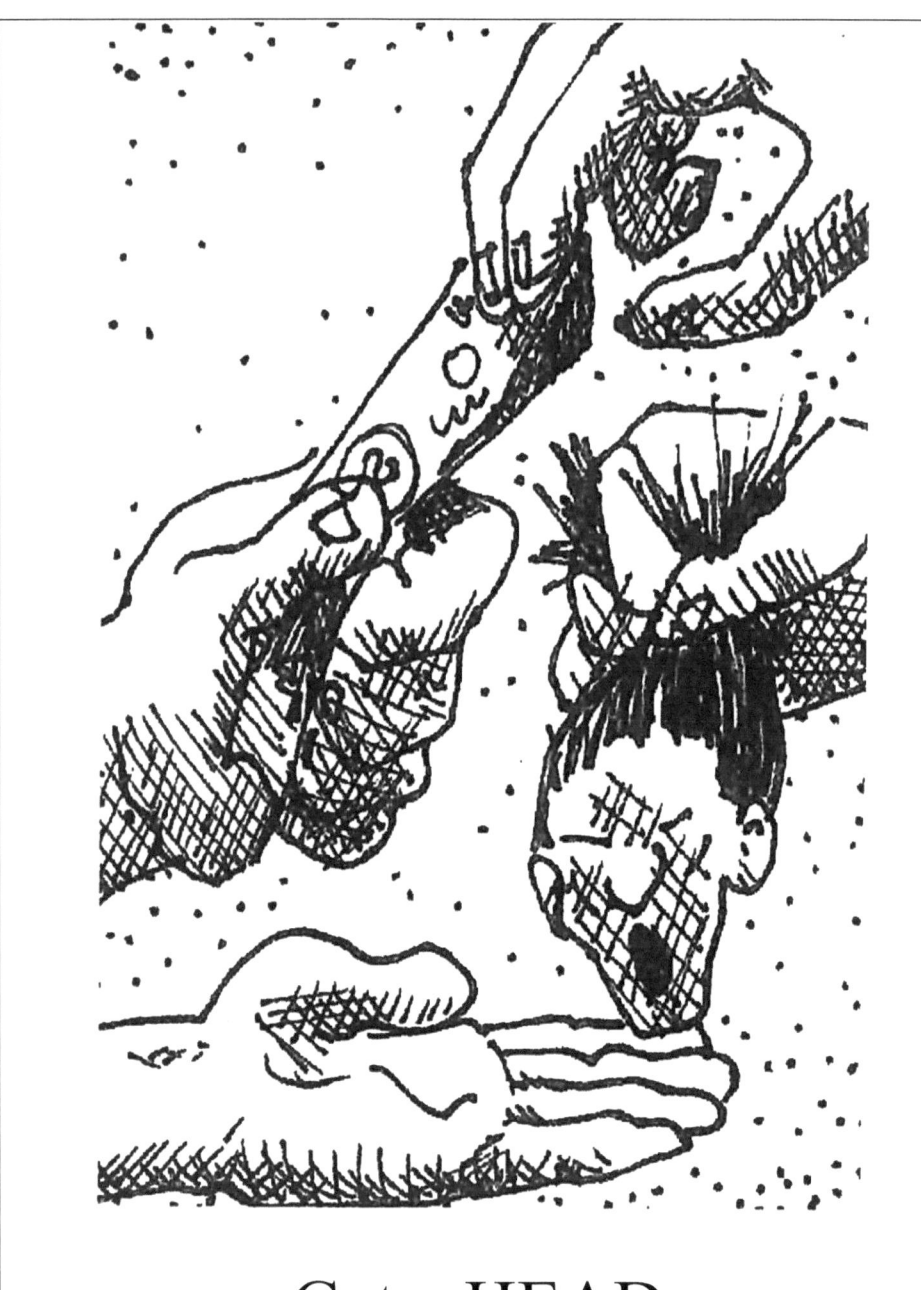

Get a HEAD

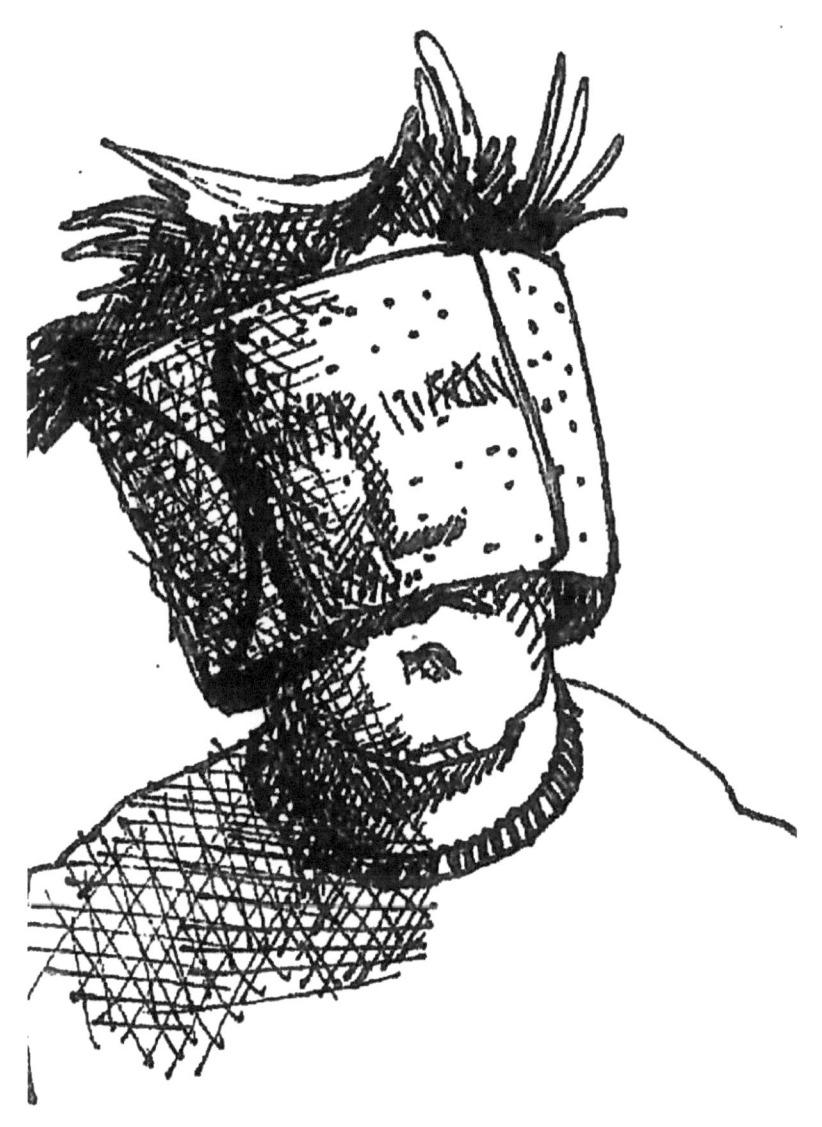

Head-ache (number one)

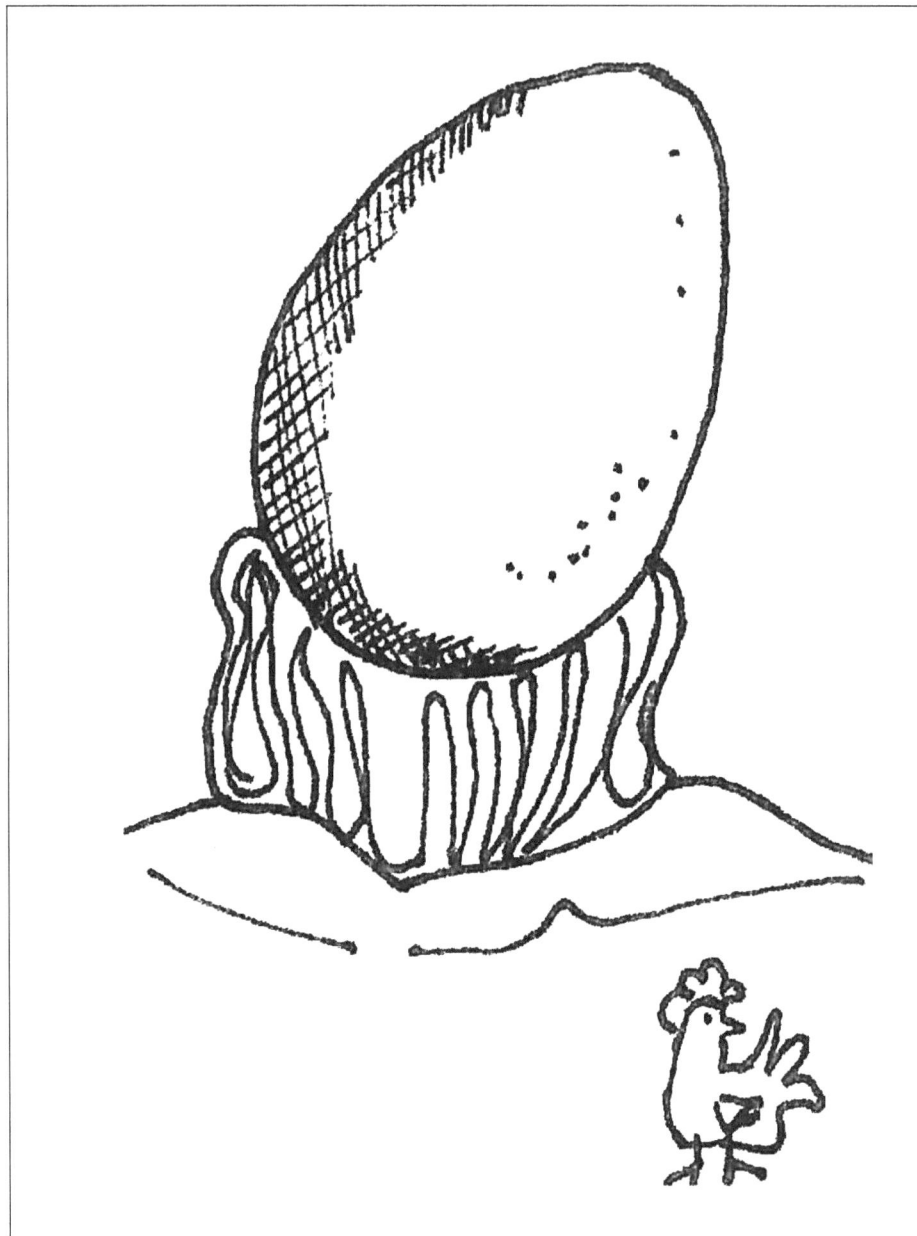

Egg Head

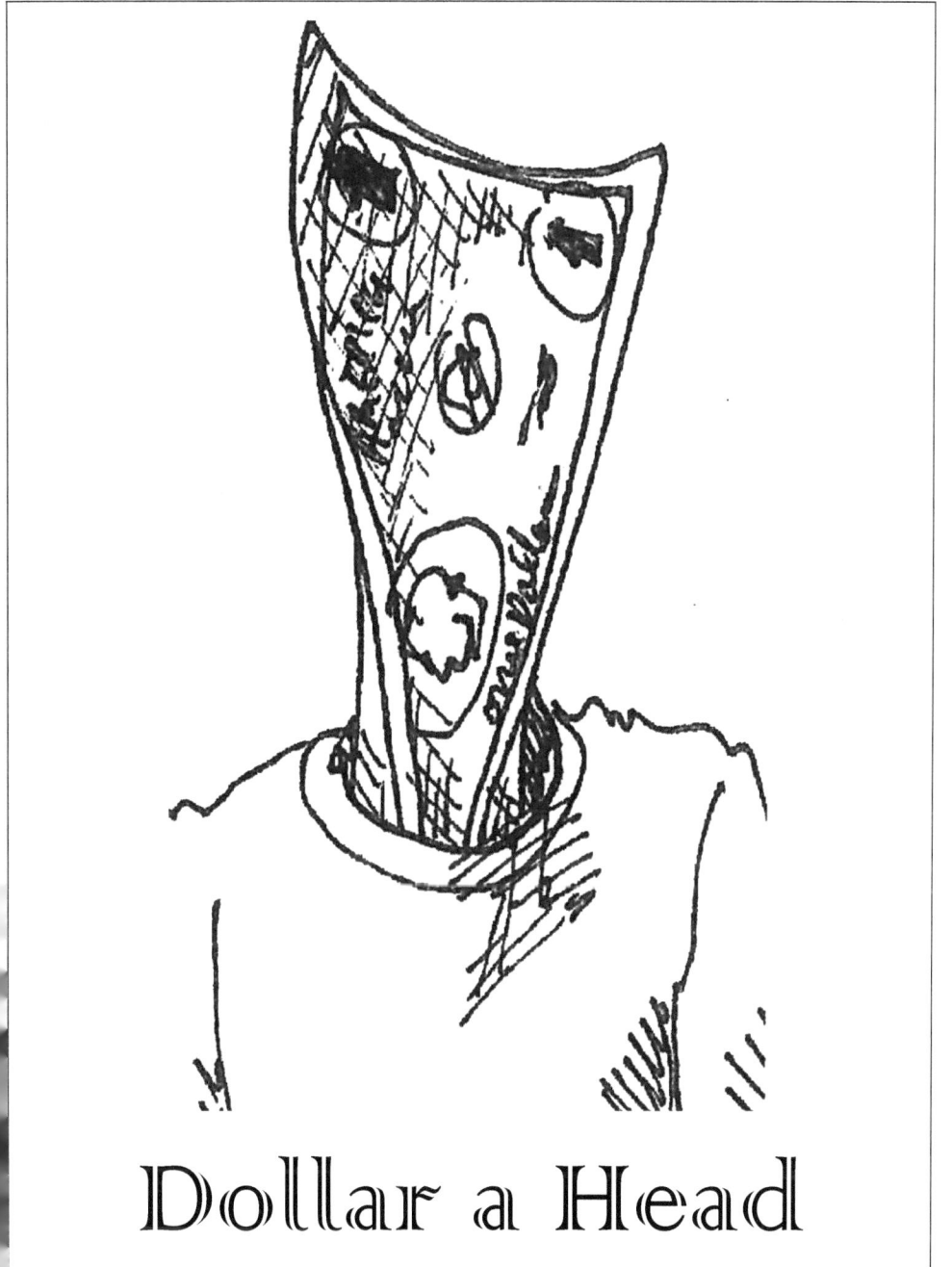

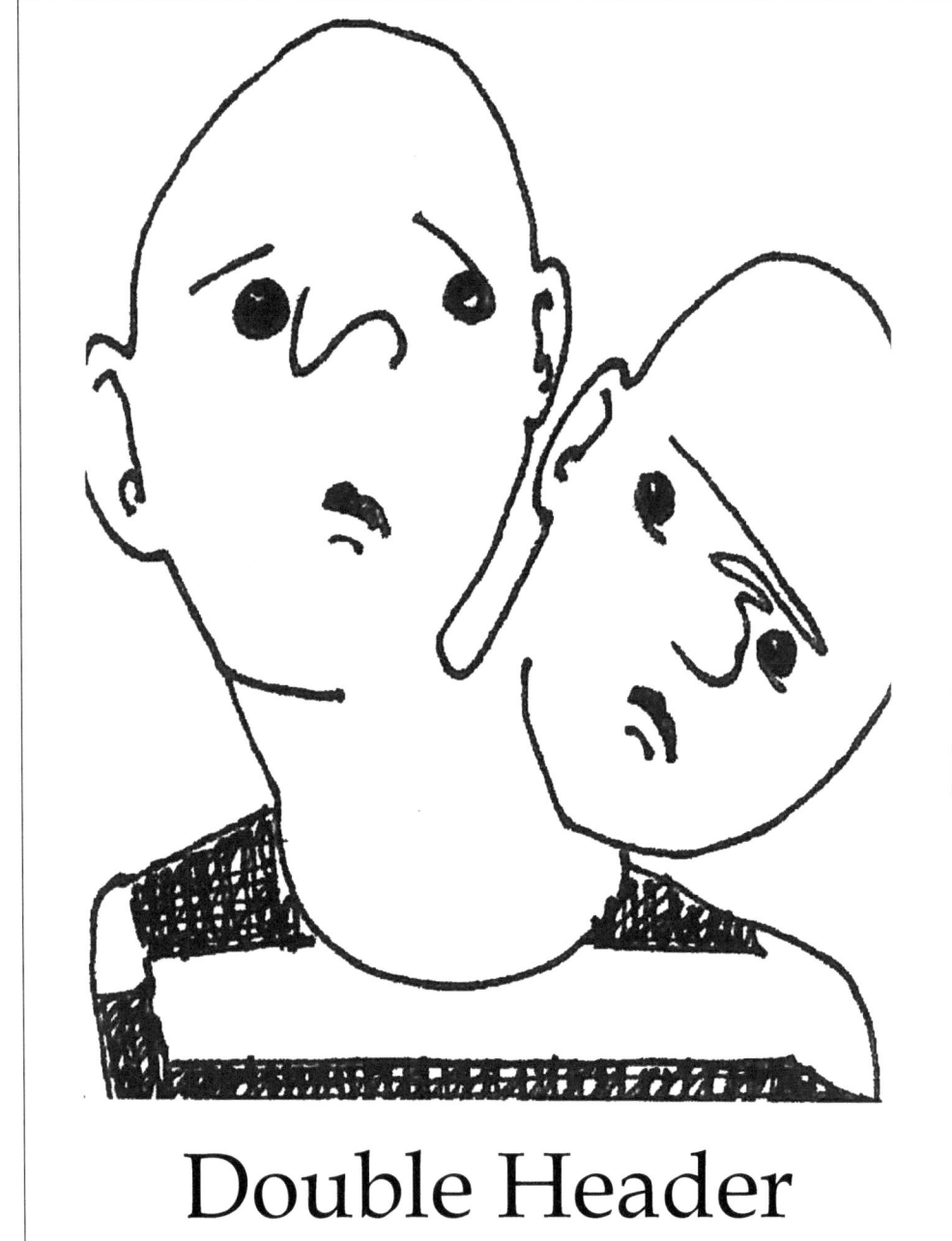

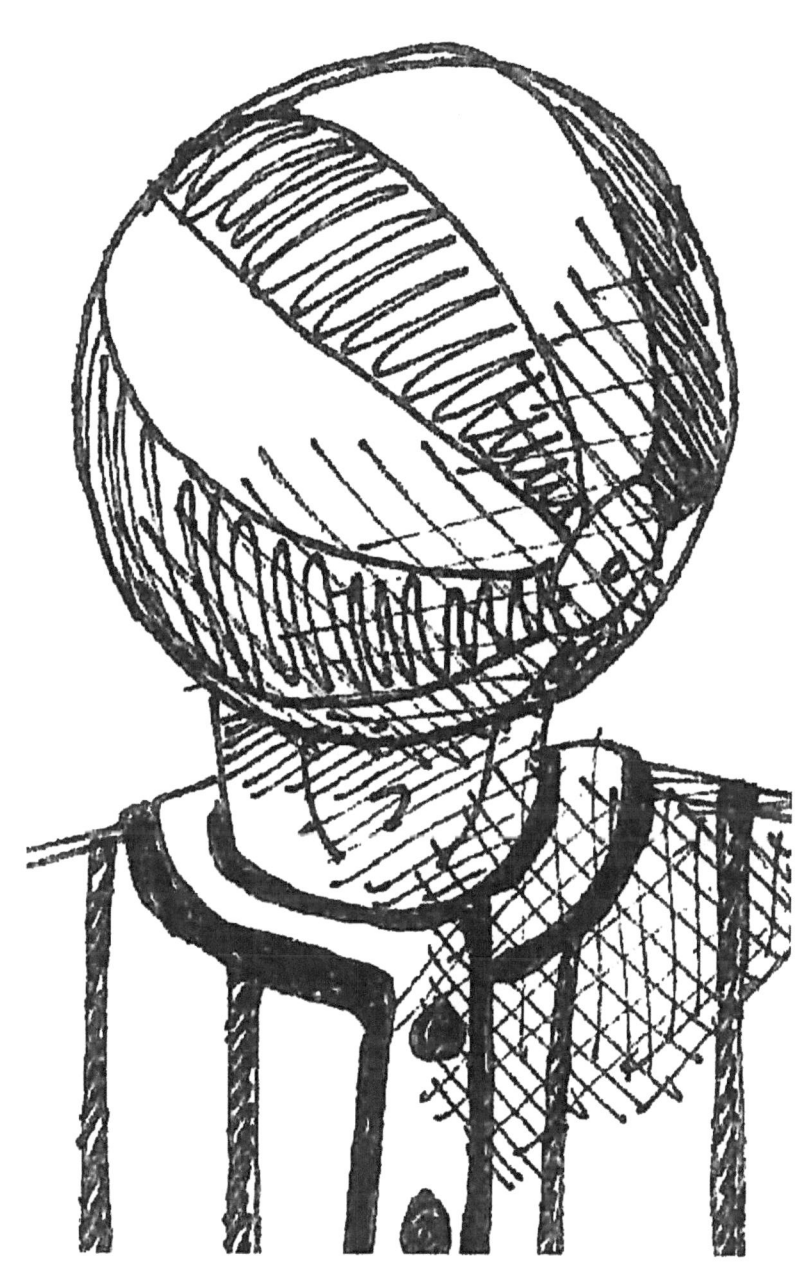

Headball

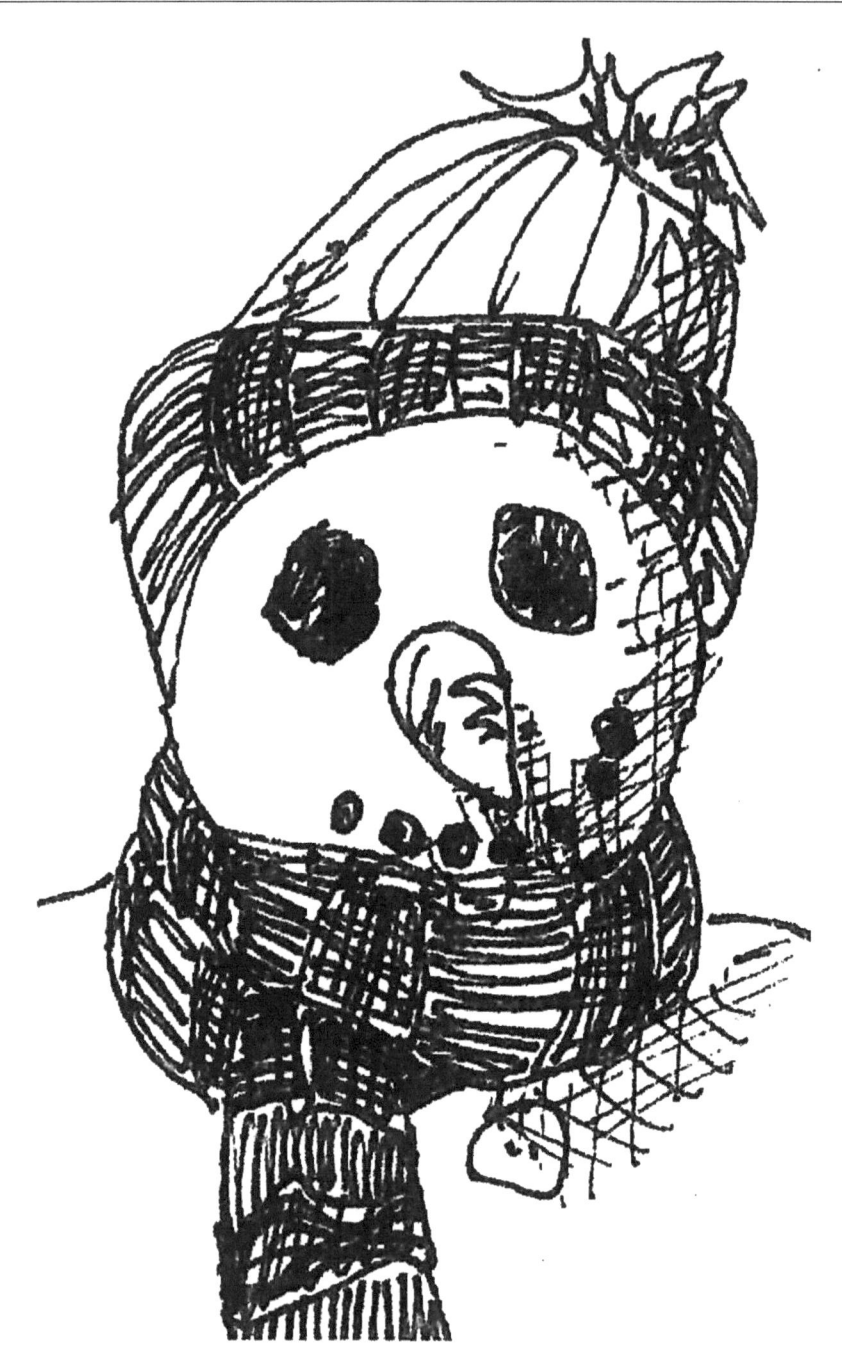

Headcold (number 2)

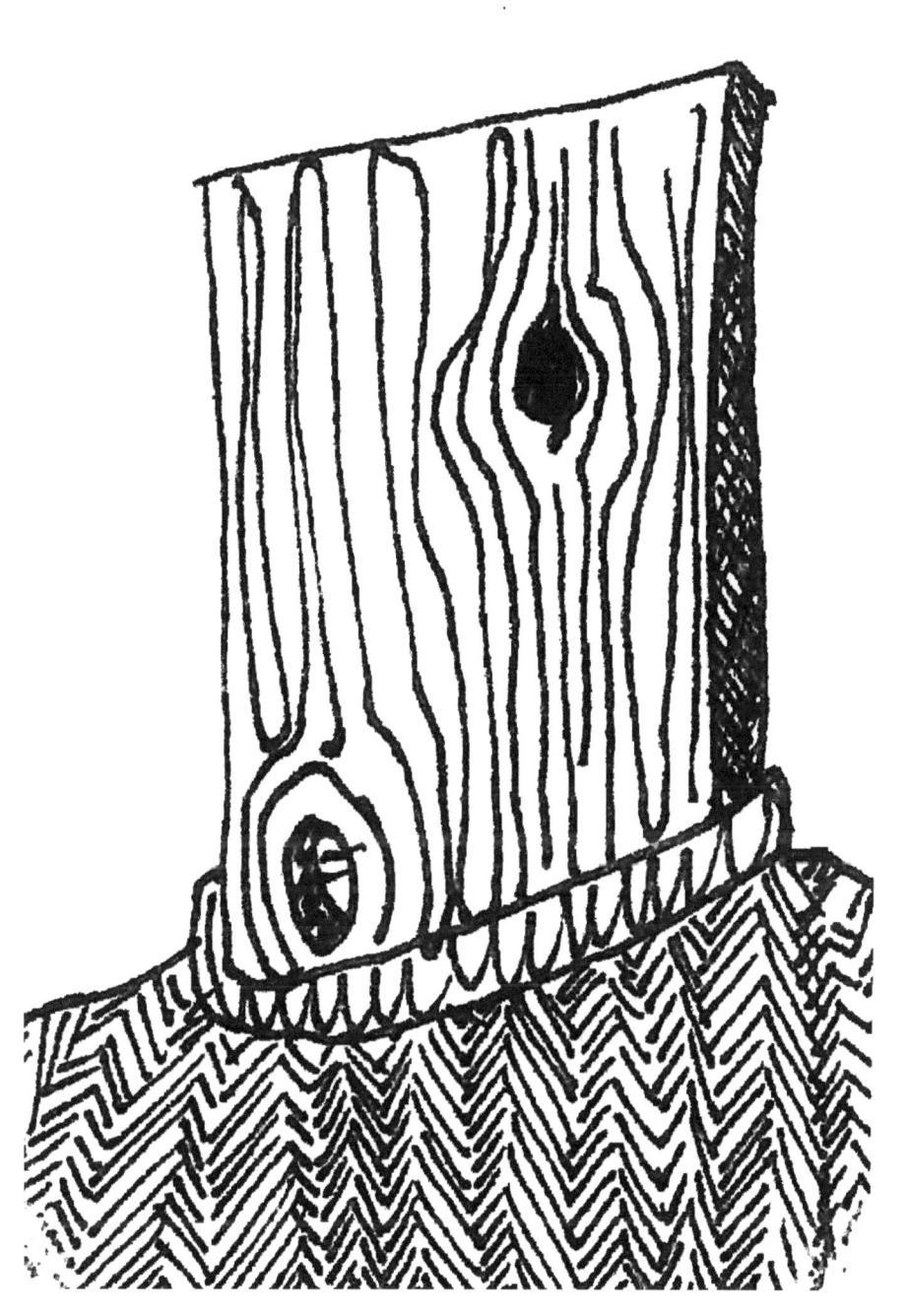

Headboard

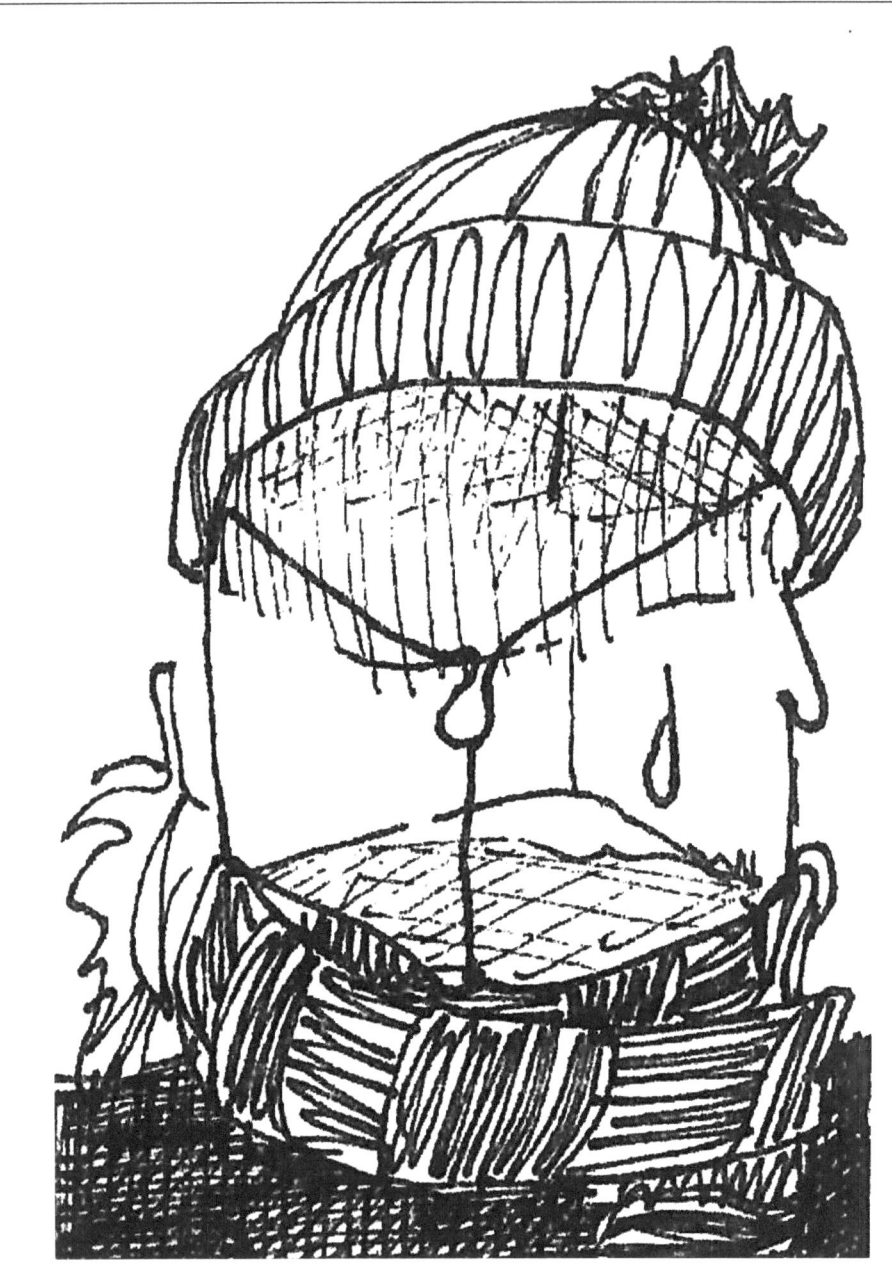

Headcold (number 1)

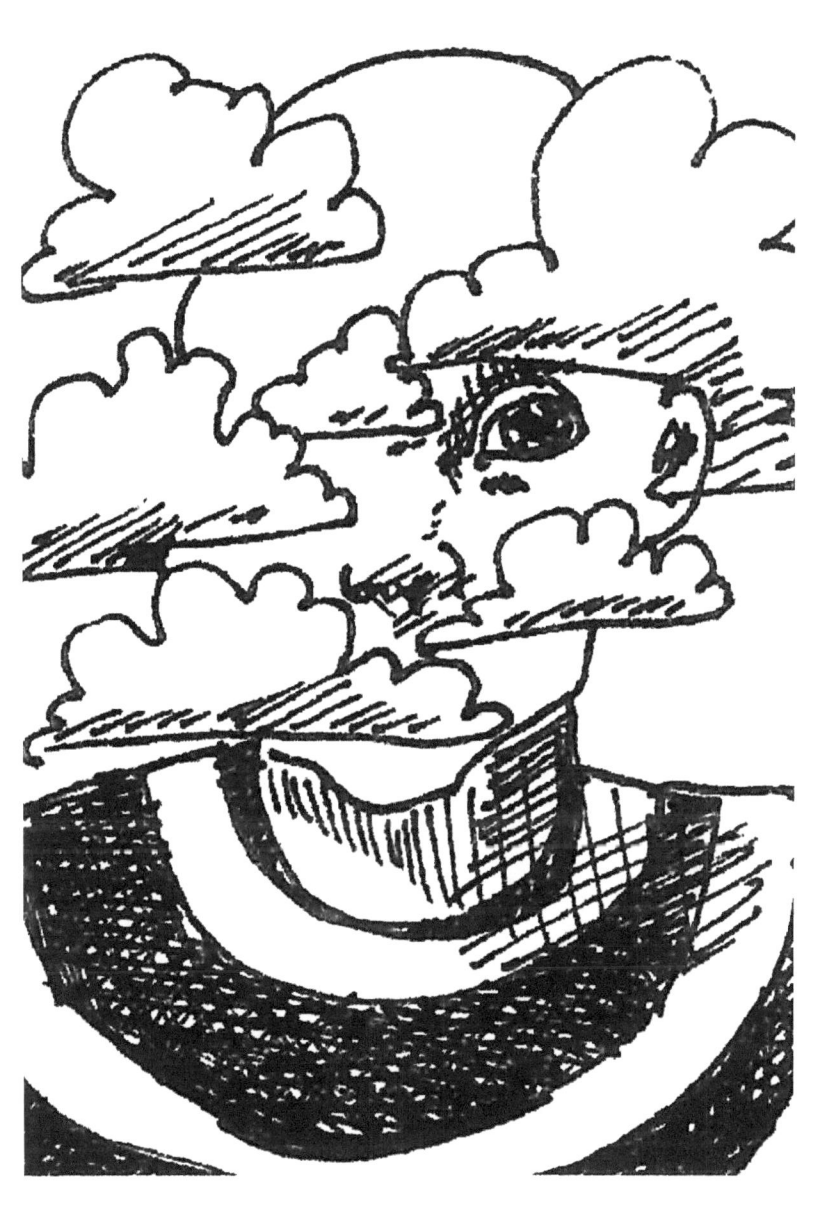

Head in the Clouds

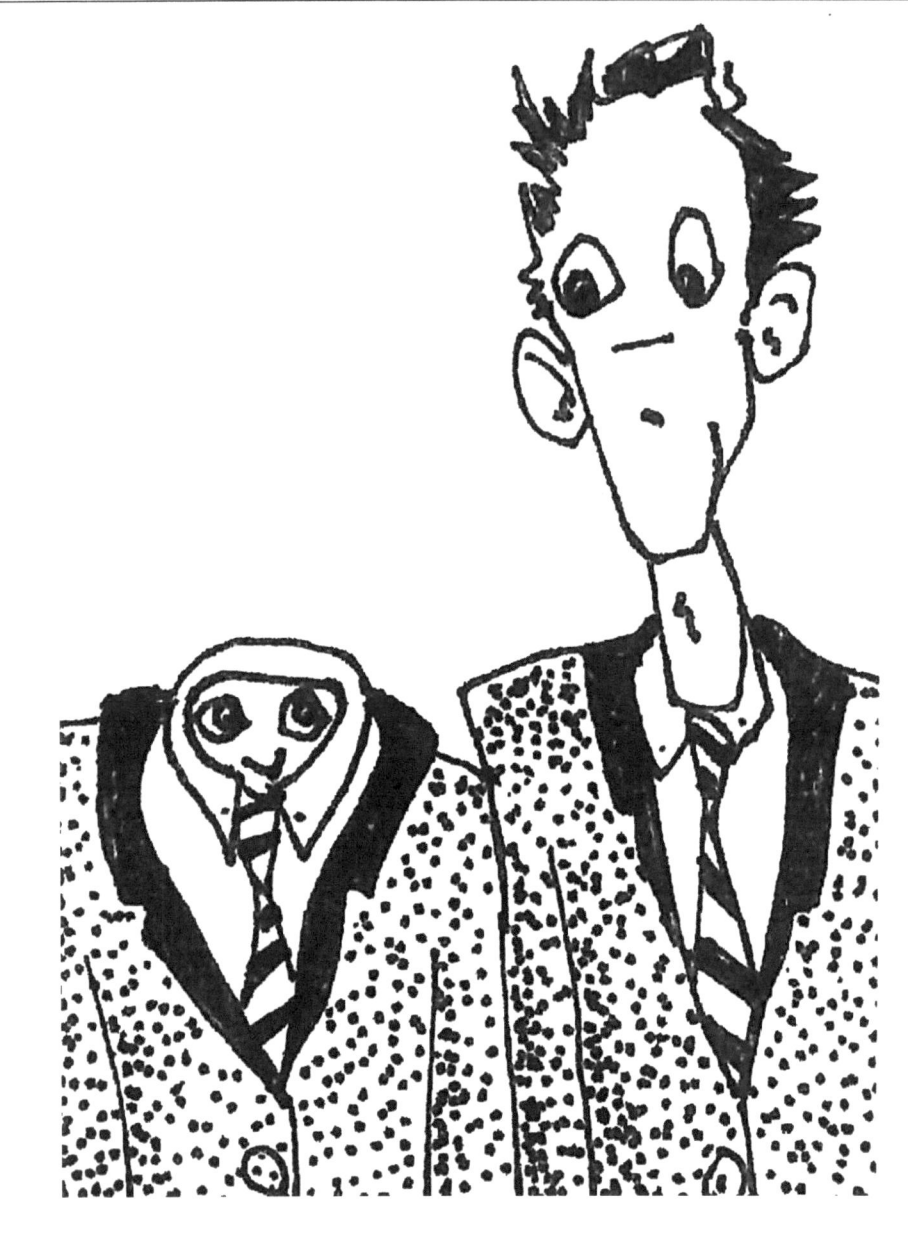

Head OUT/Head IN

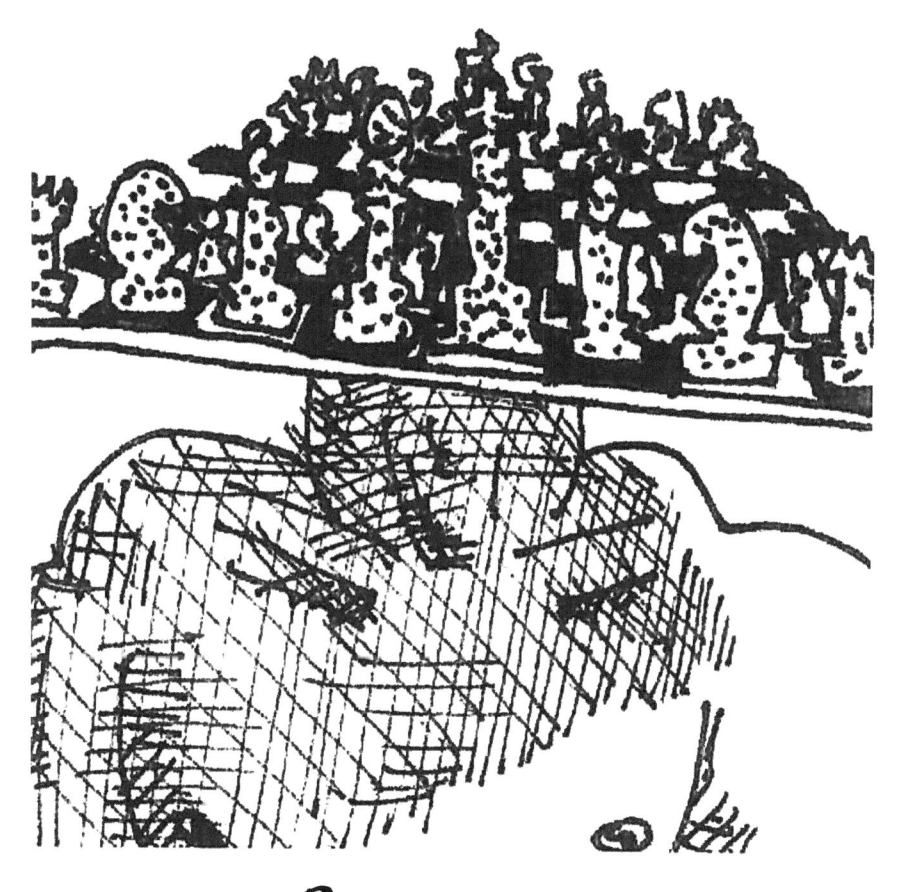

Head Game

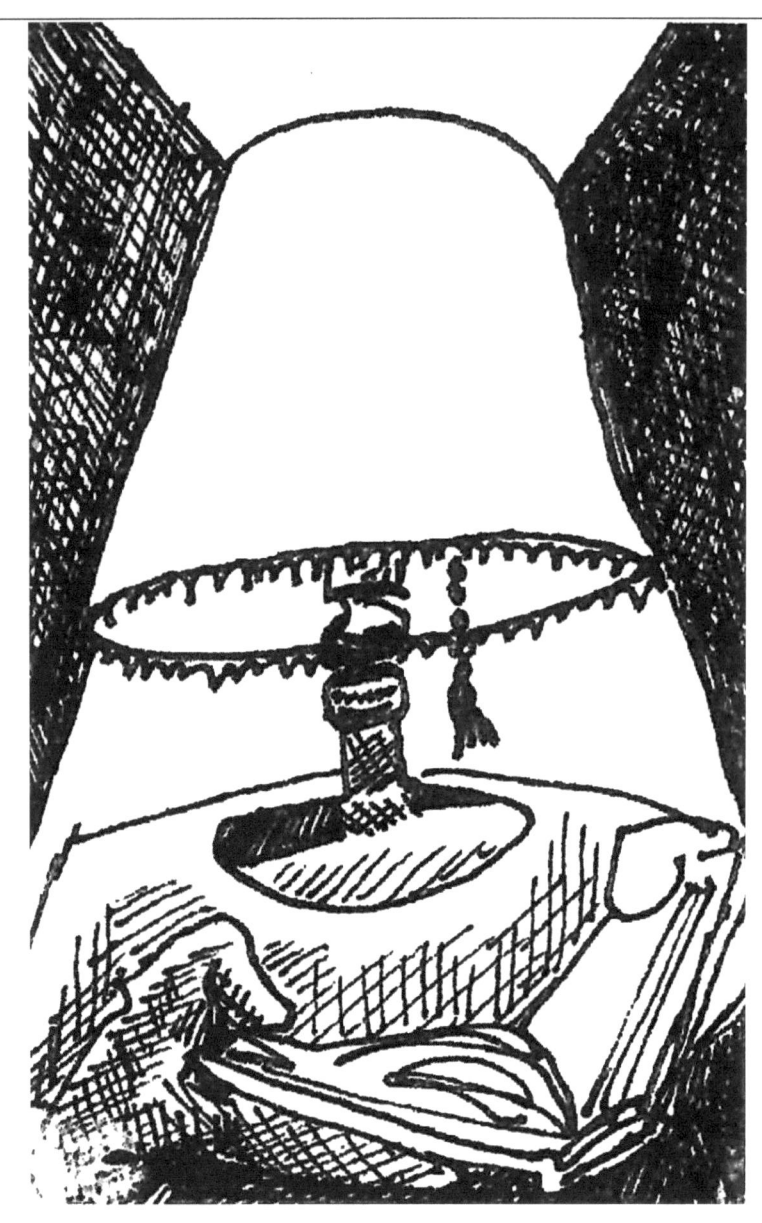

Headlamp

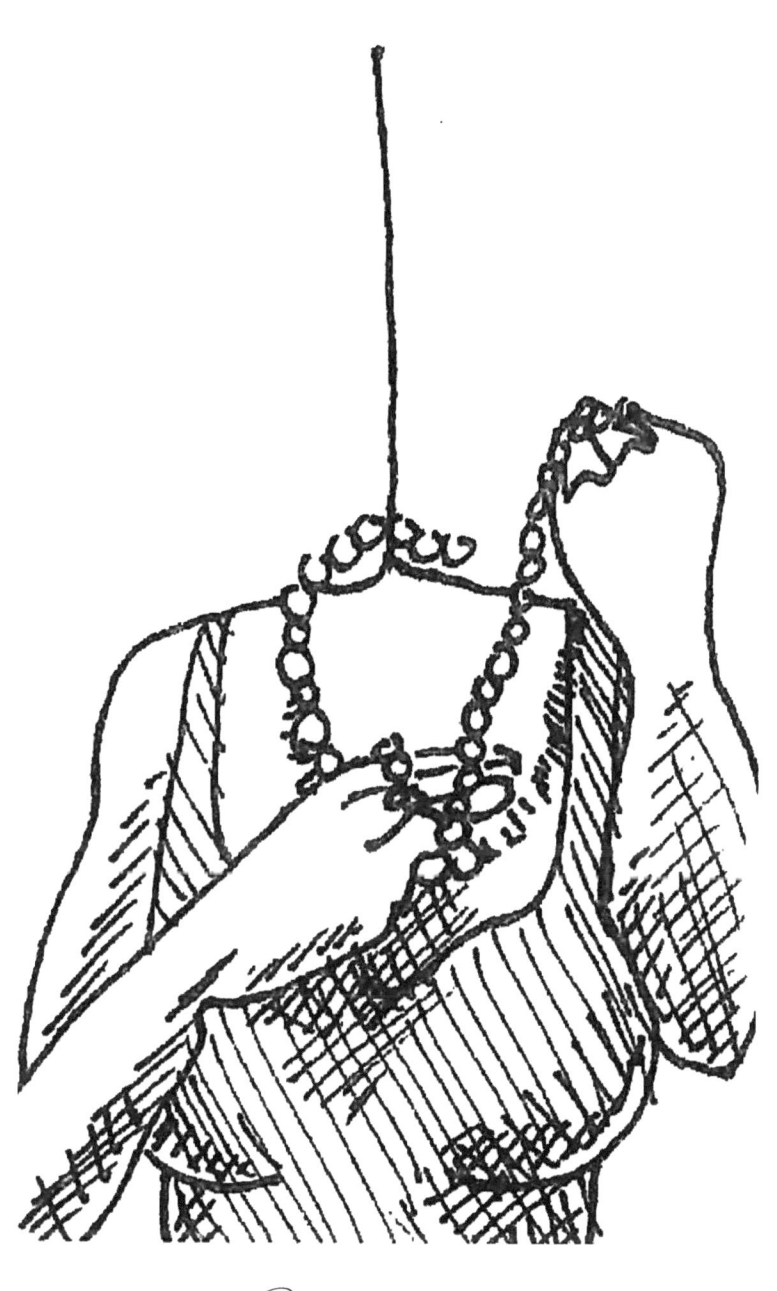

Headline

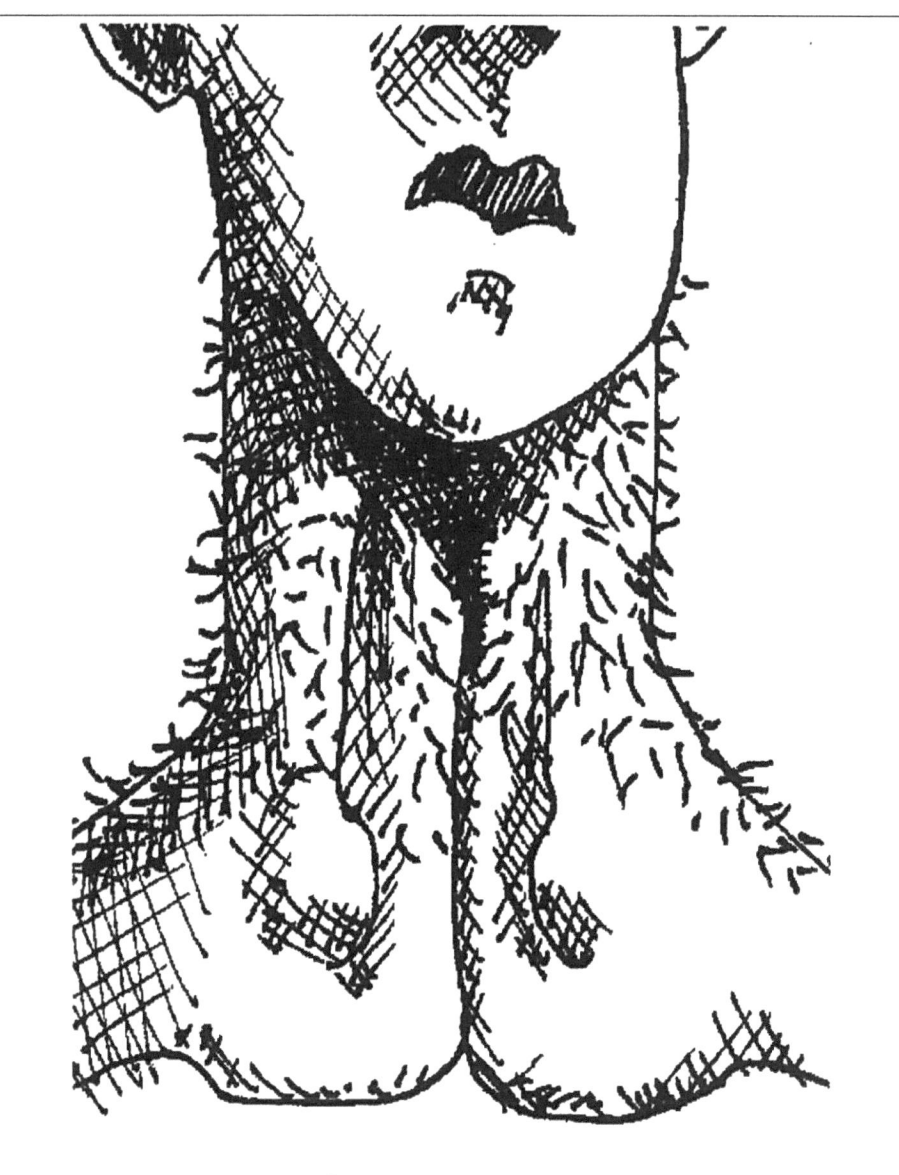

Head Over Heels

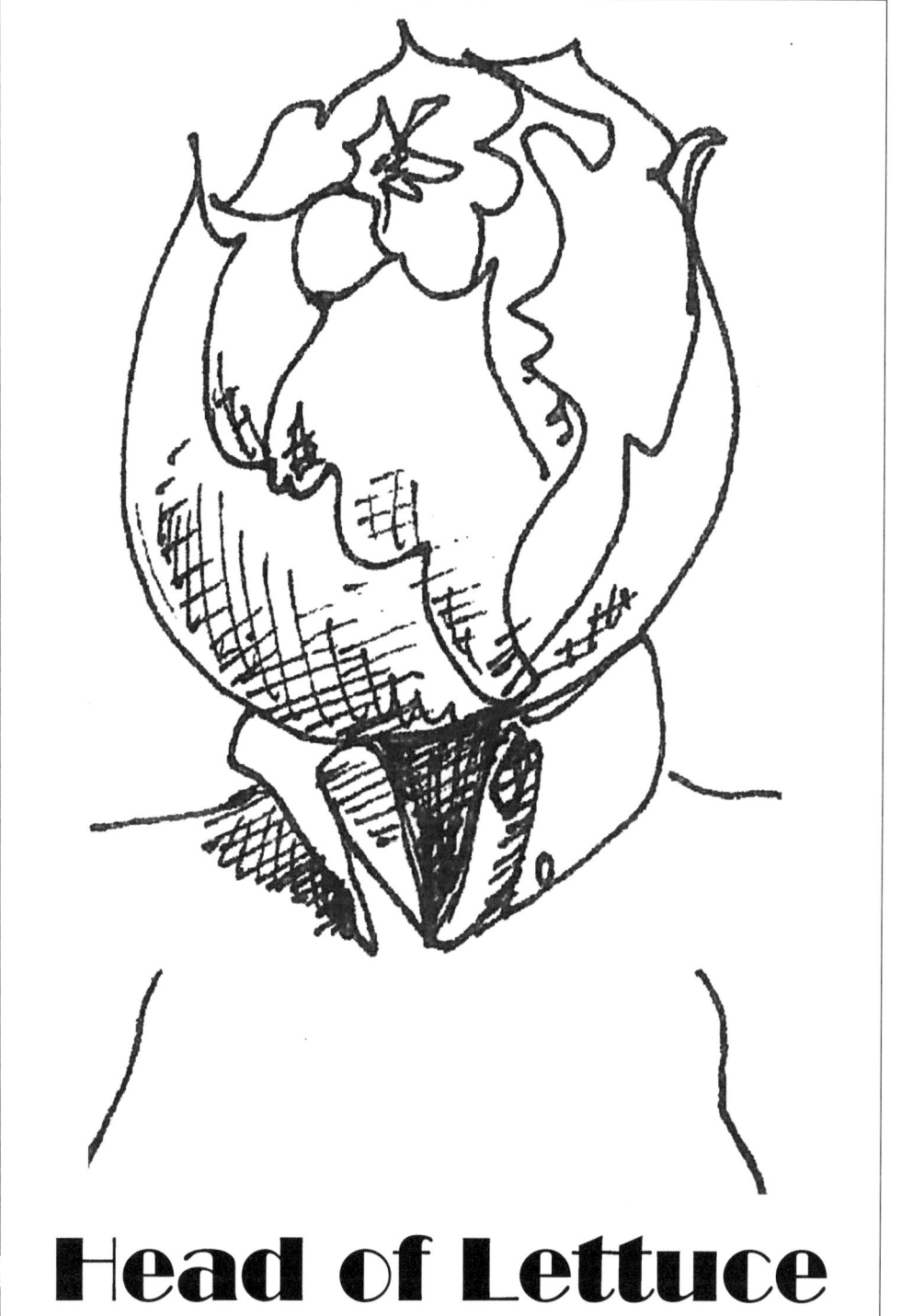

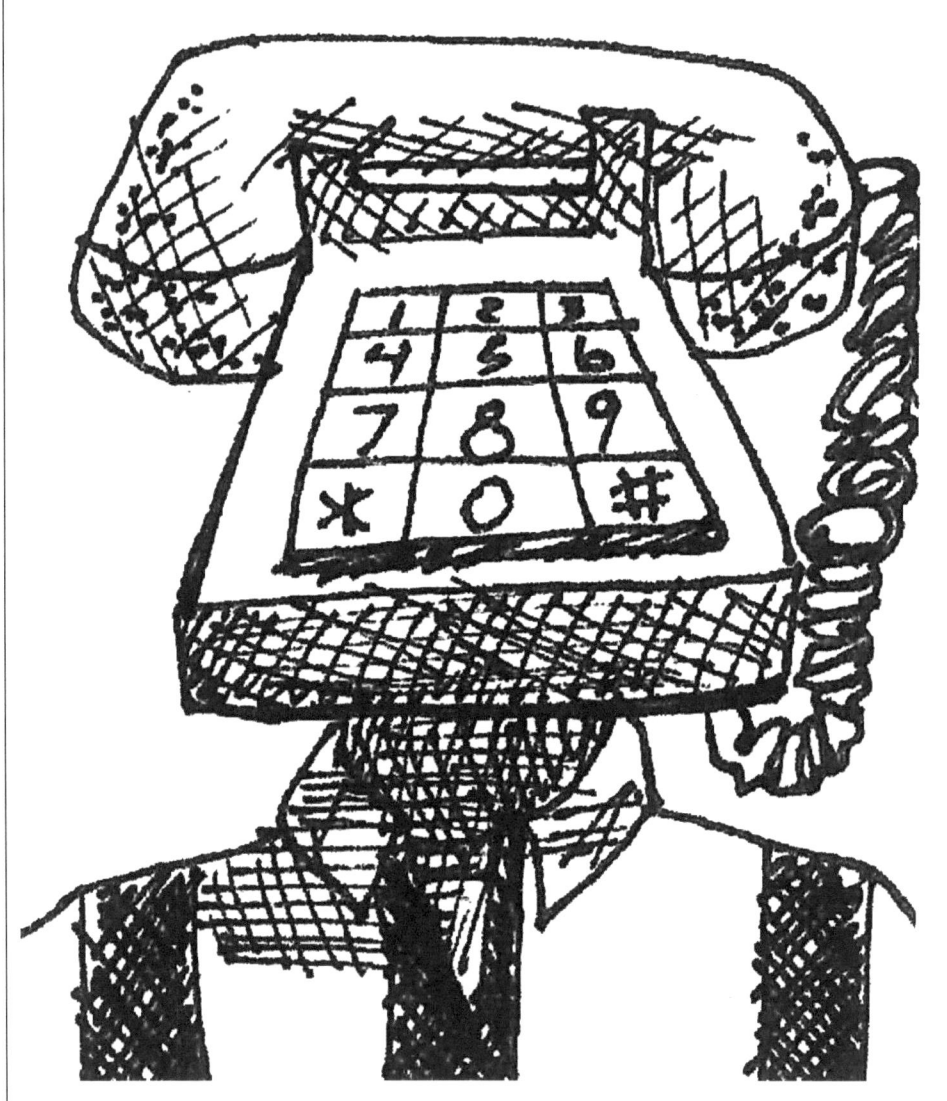

Headphone

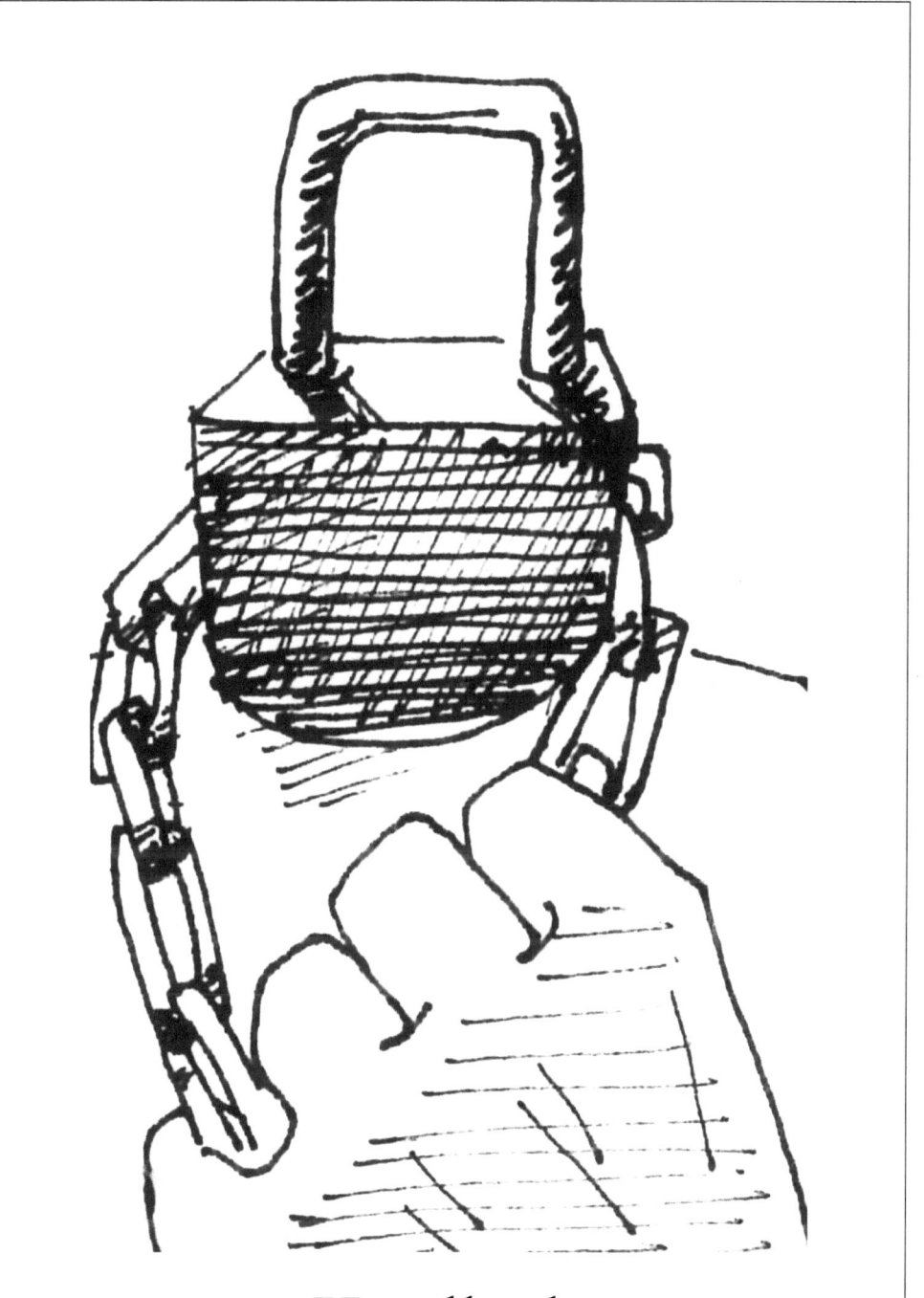

Headlock

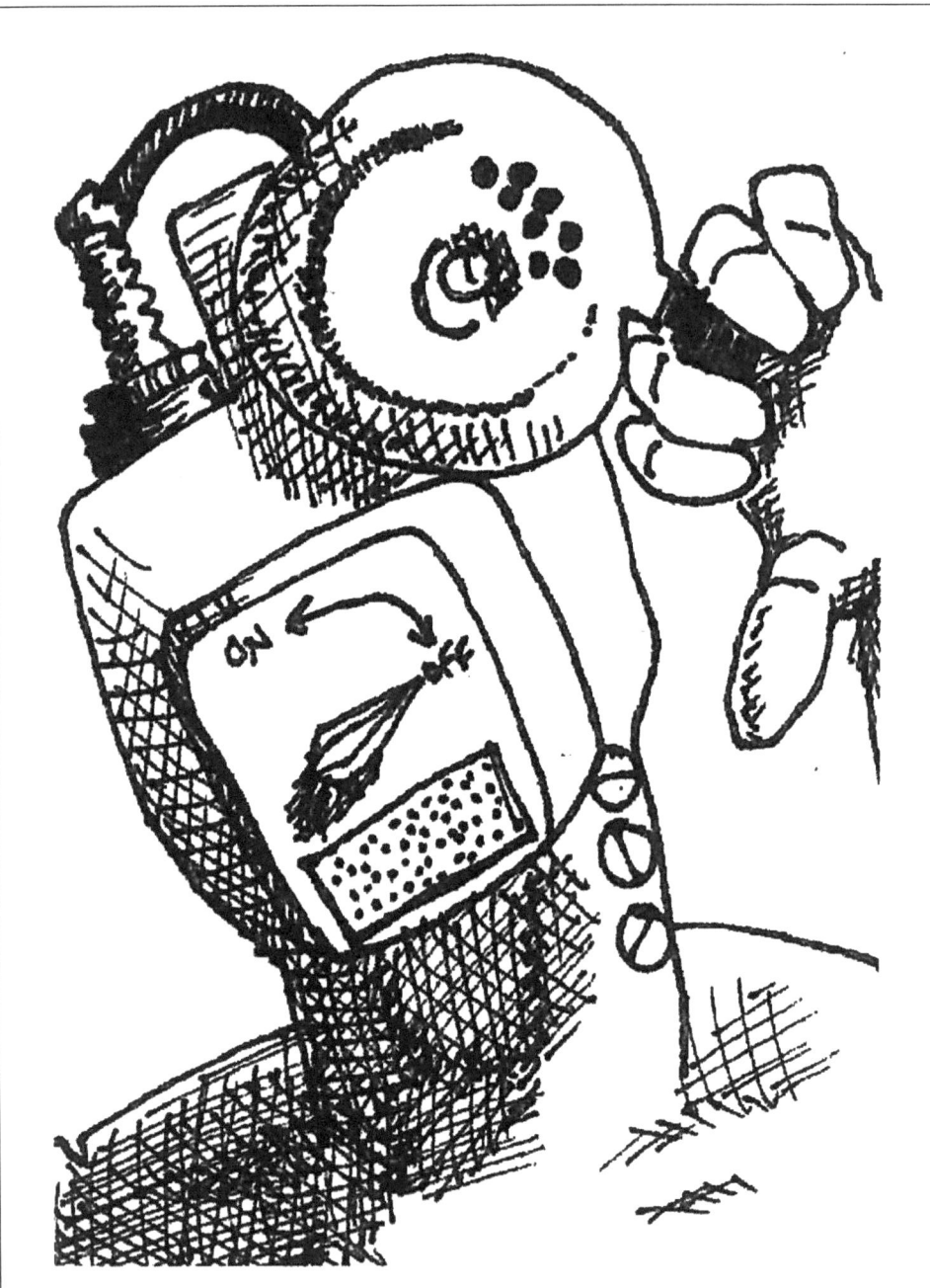

Head Start

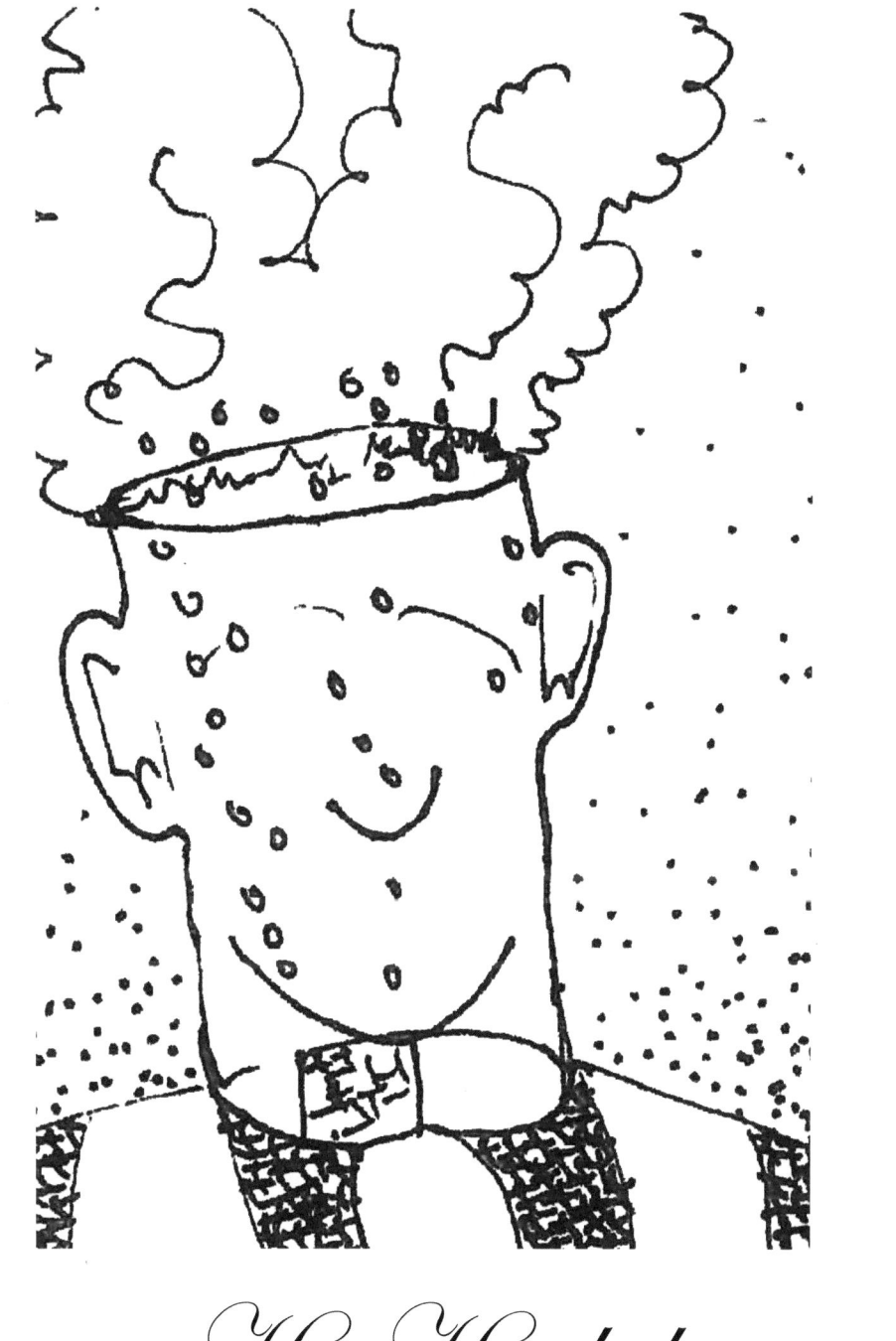

Hot Headed

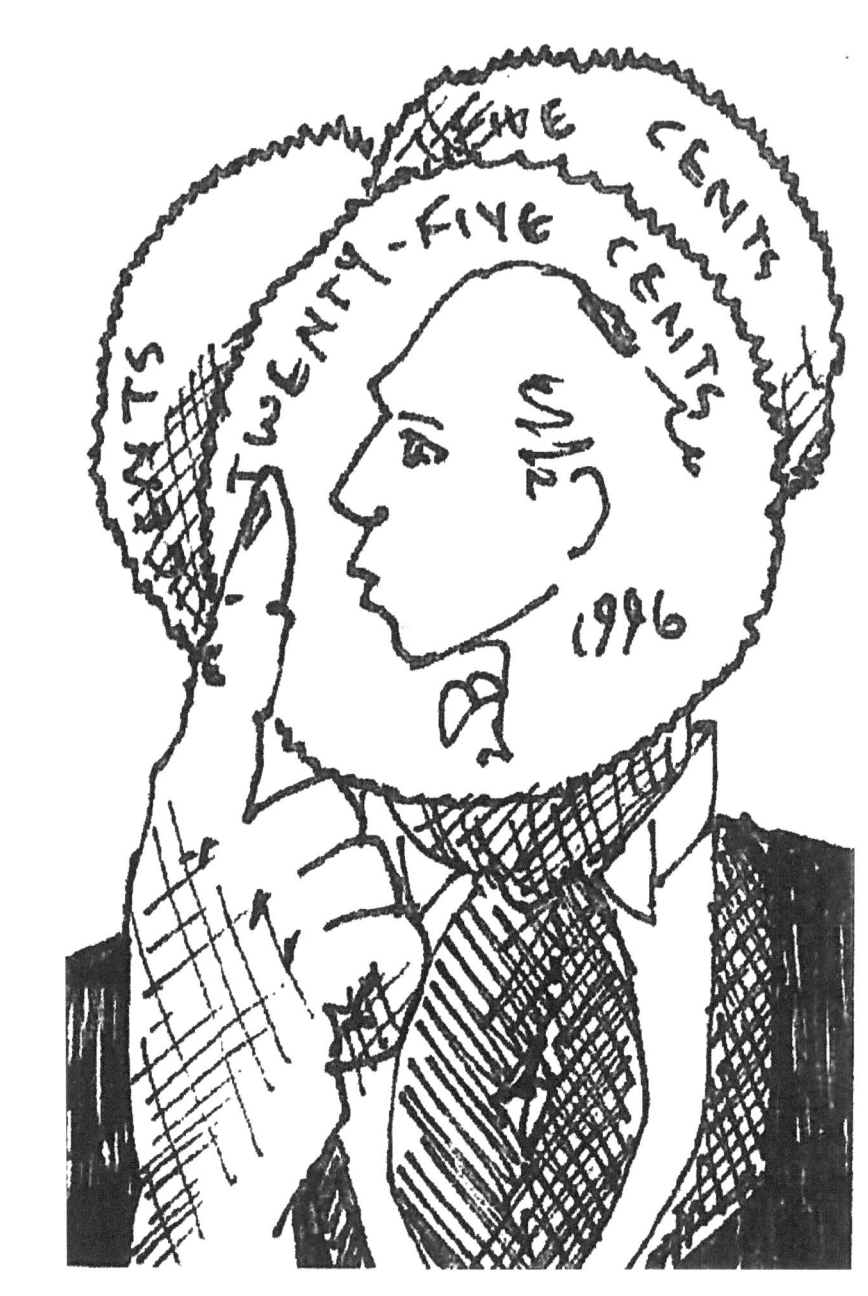

Headquarters

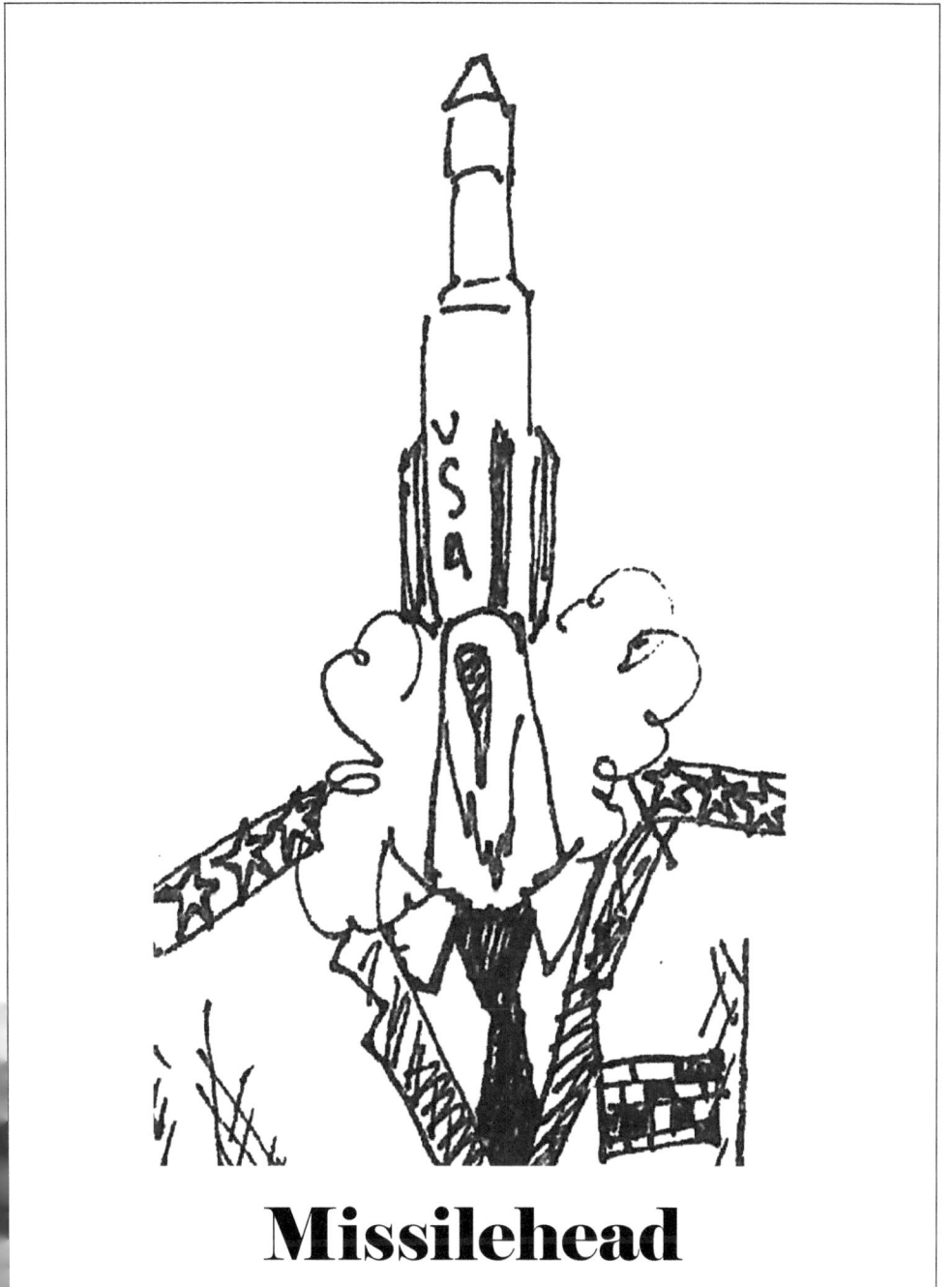

Missilehead

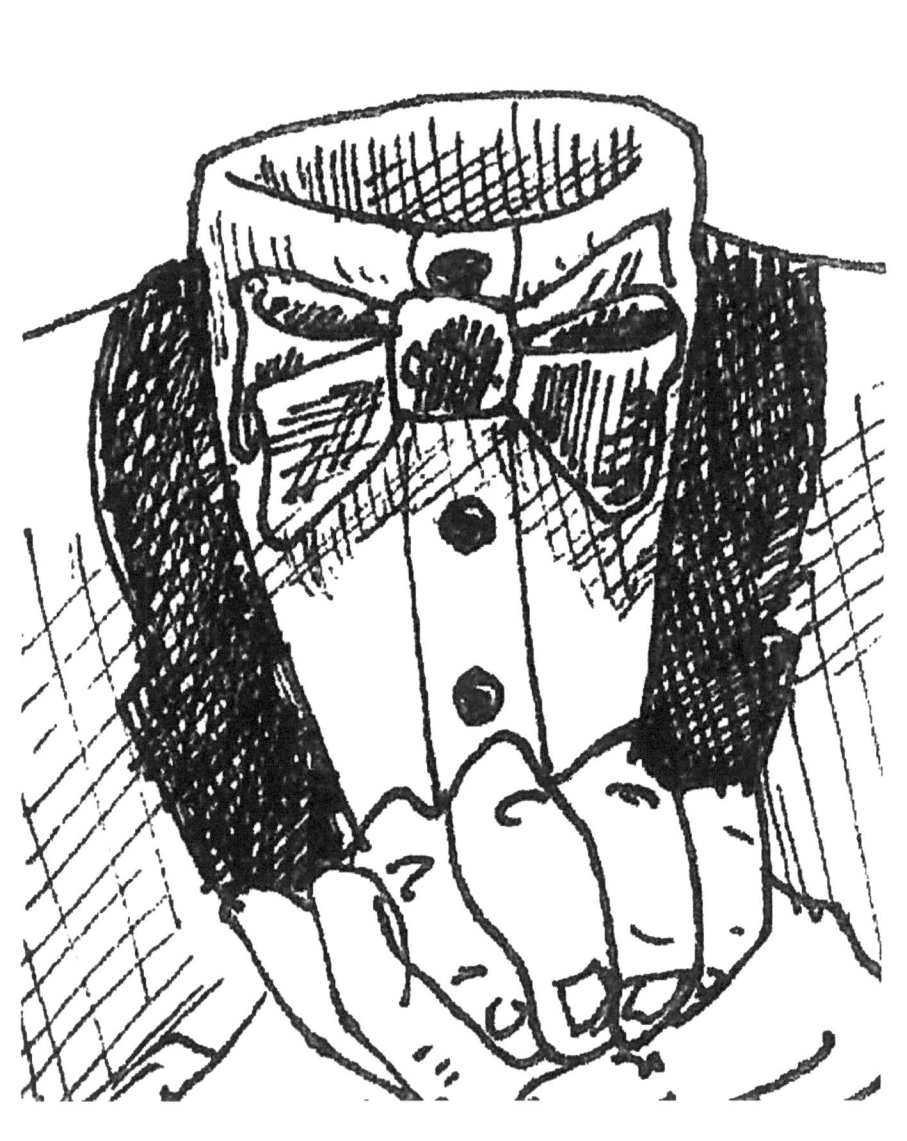

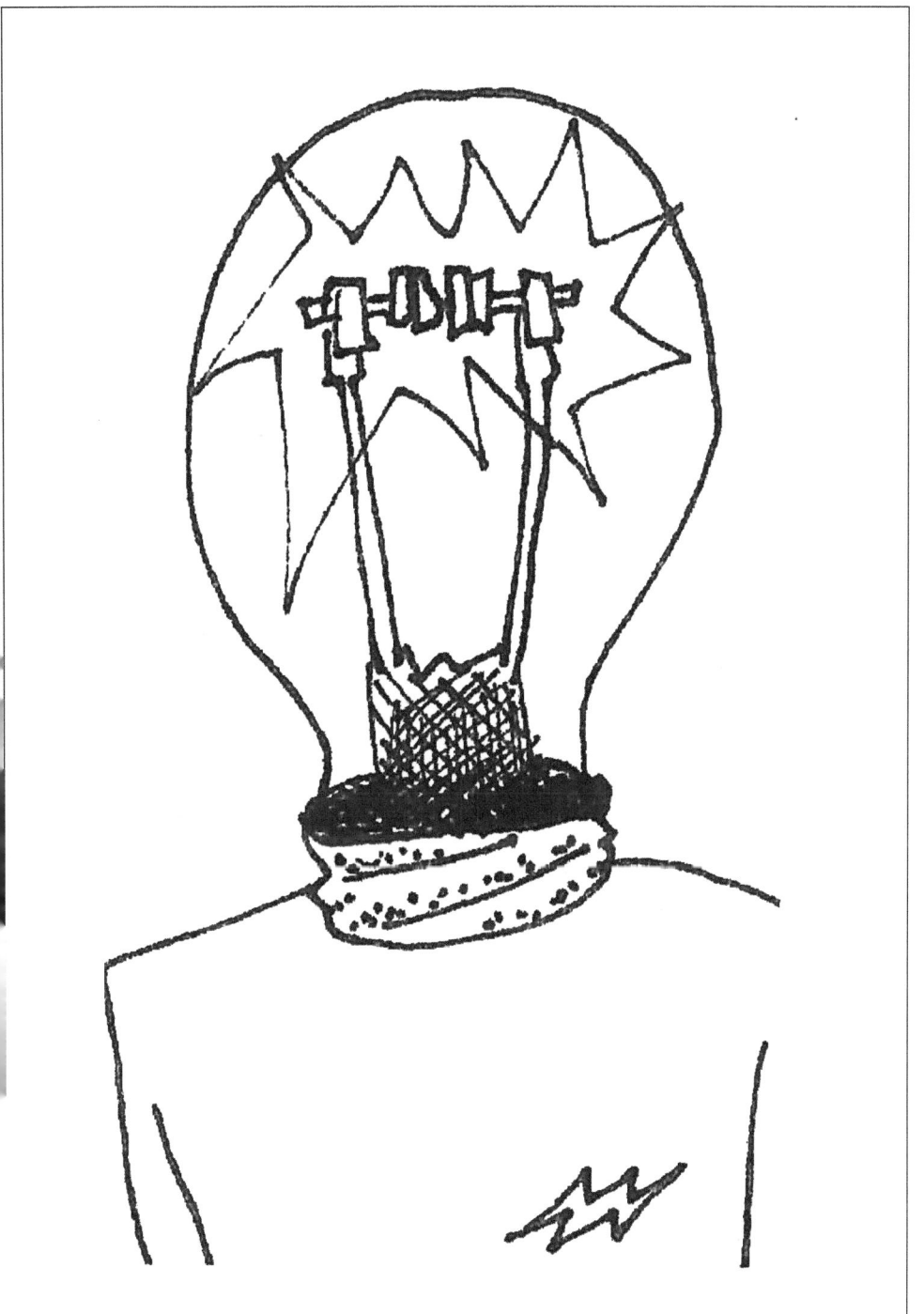

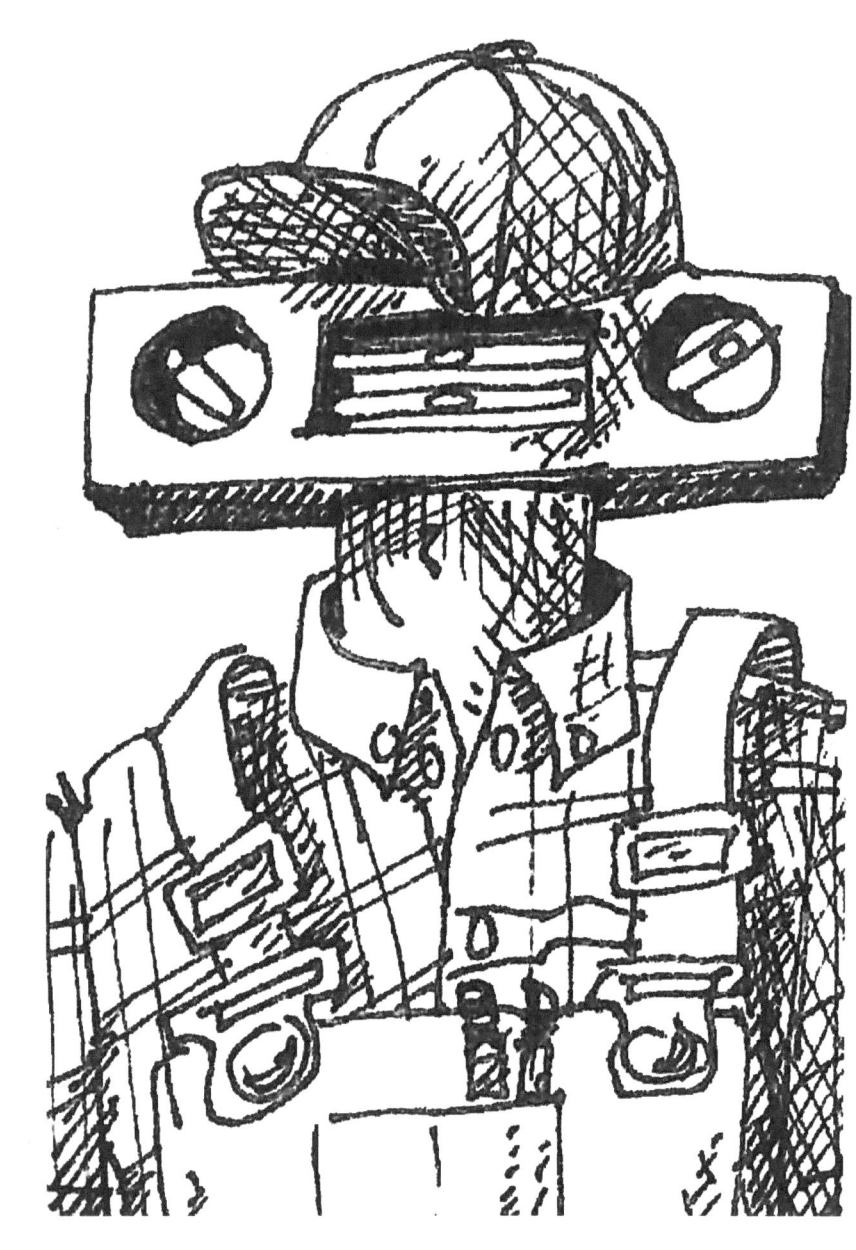

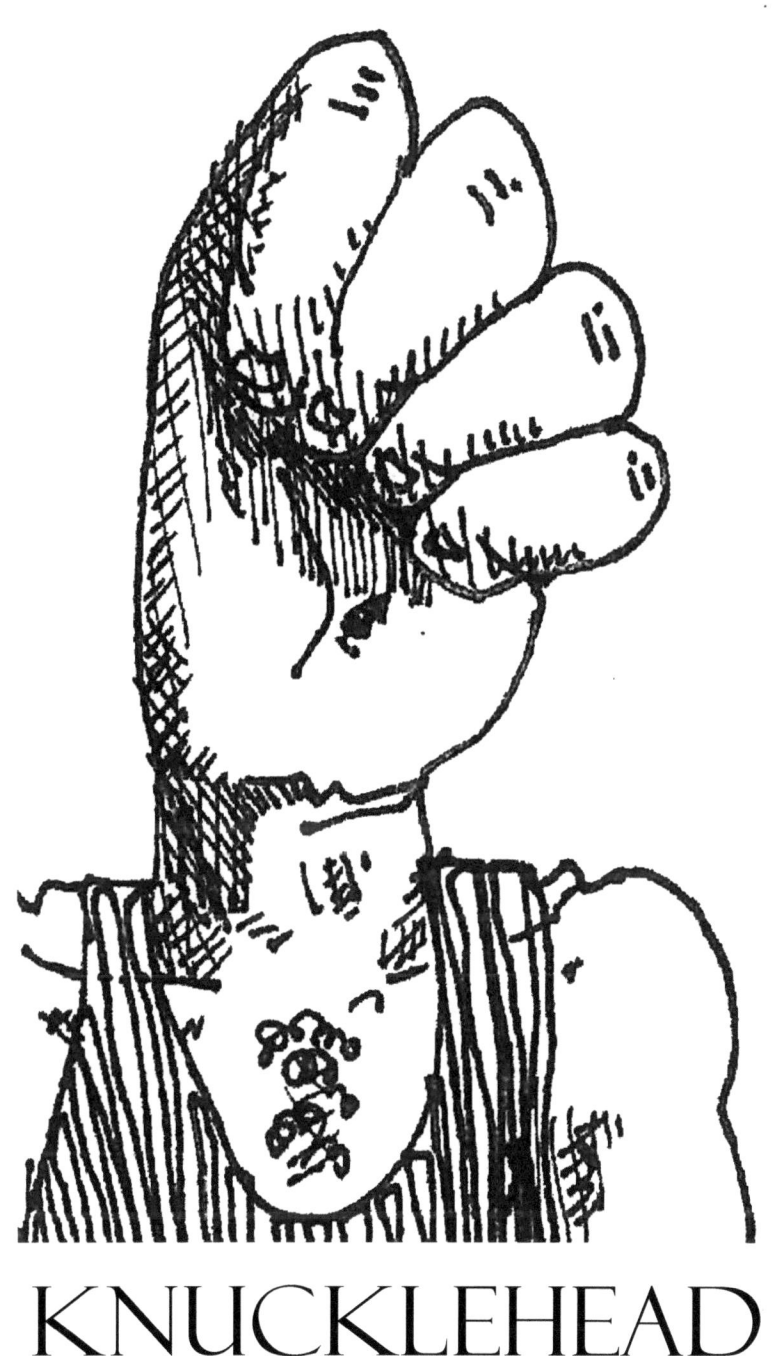

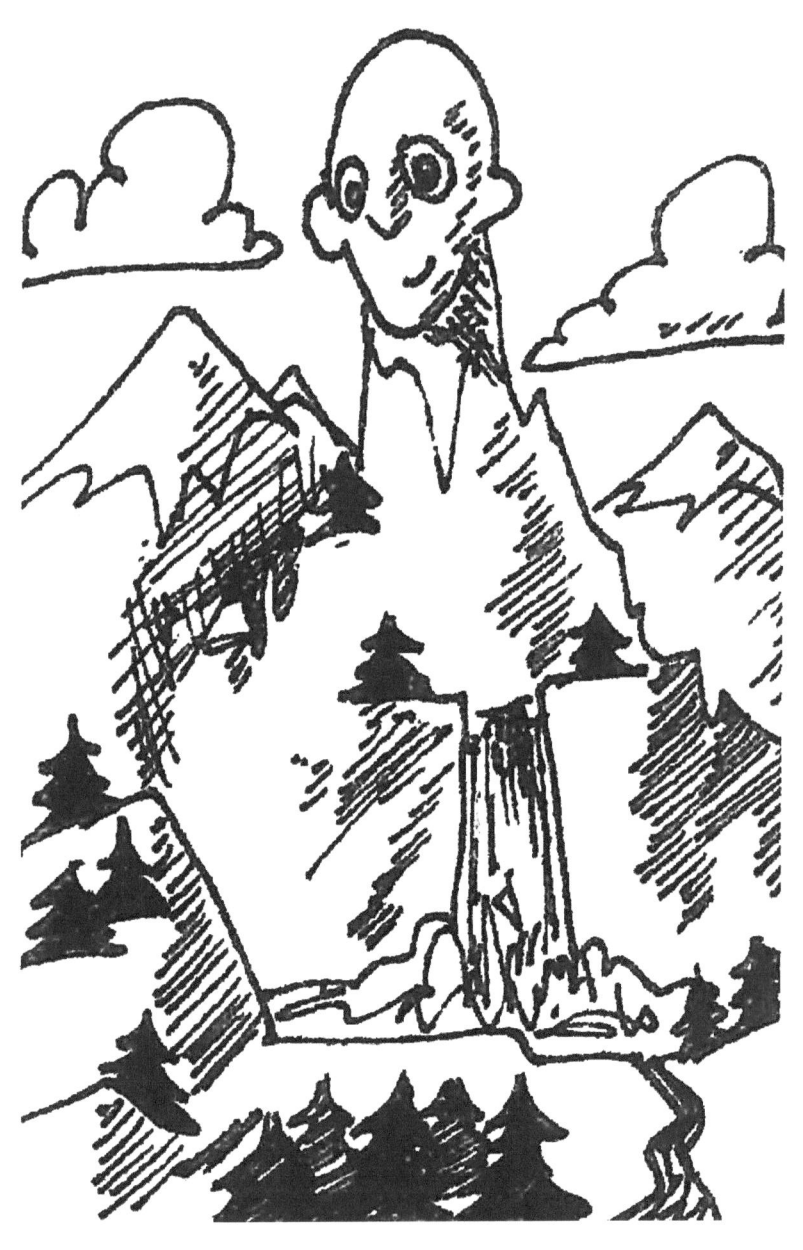

Head to the Mountains

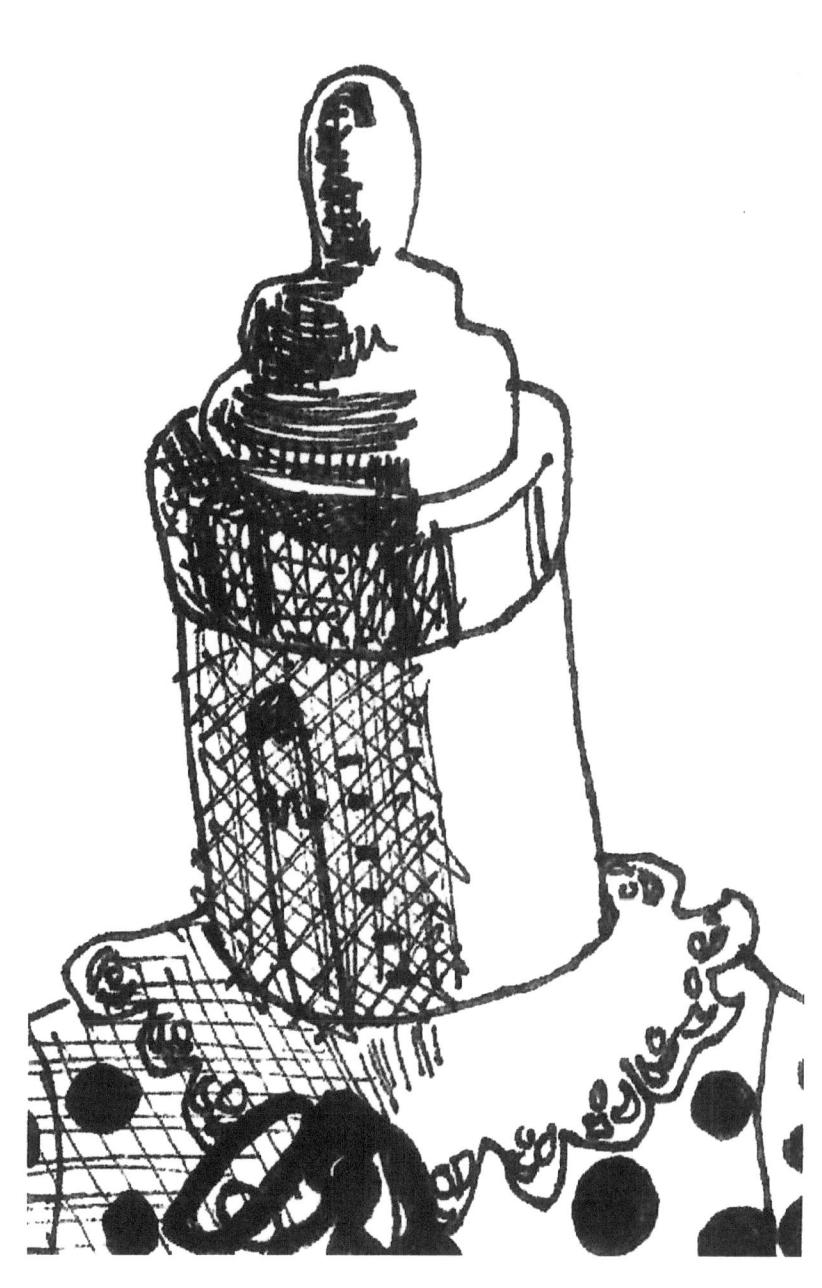

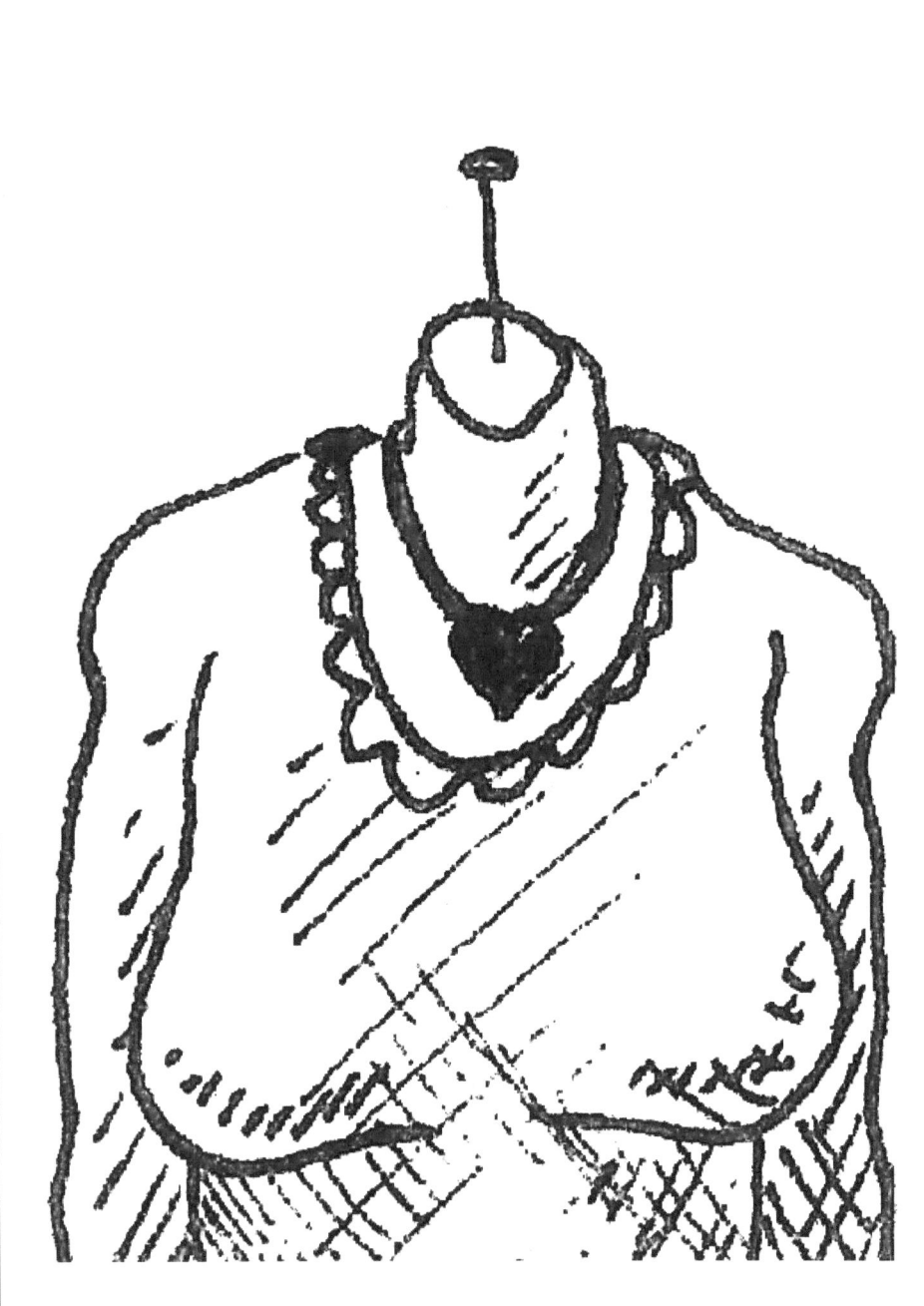

Pinhead

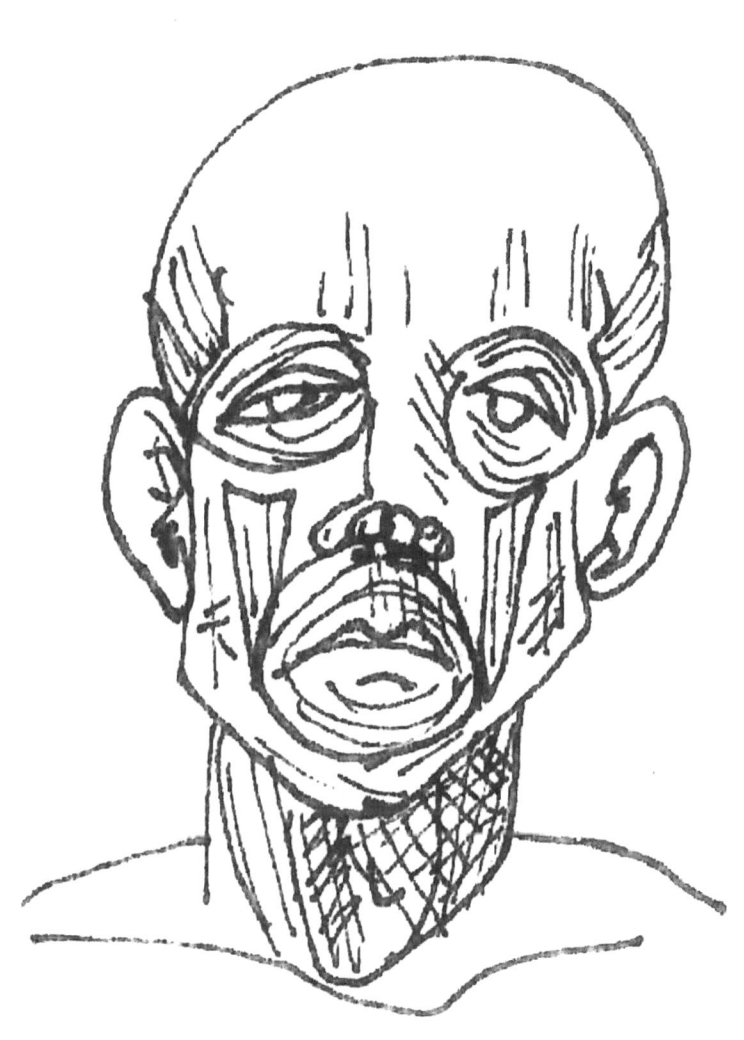

Musclehead

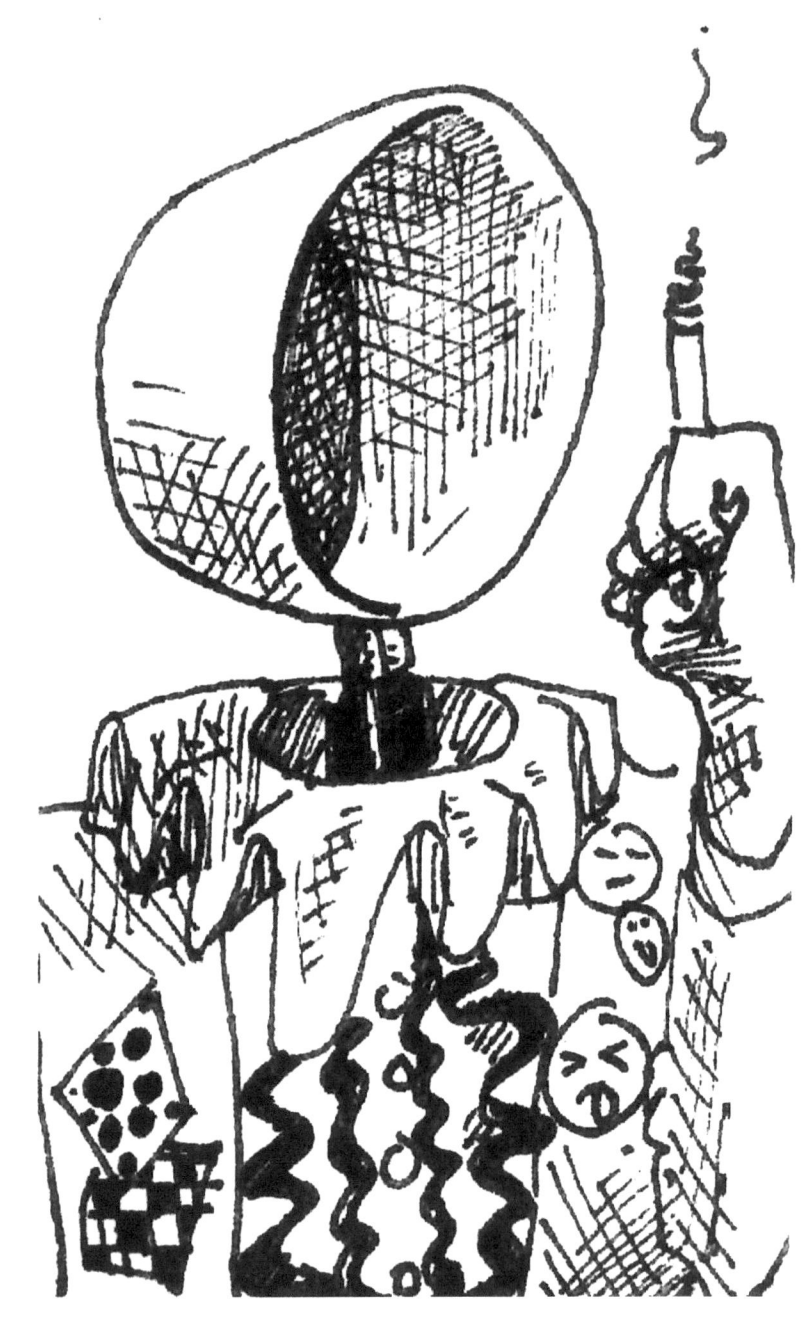

Pothead

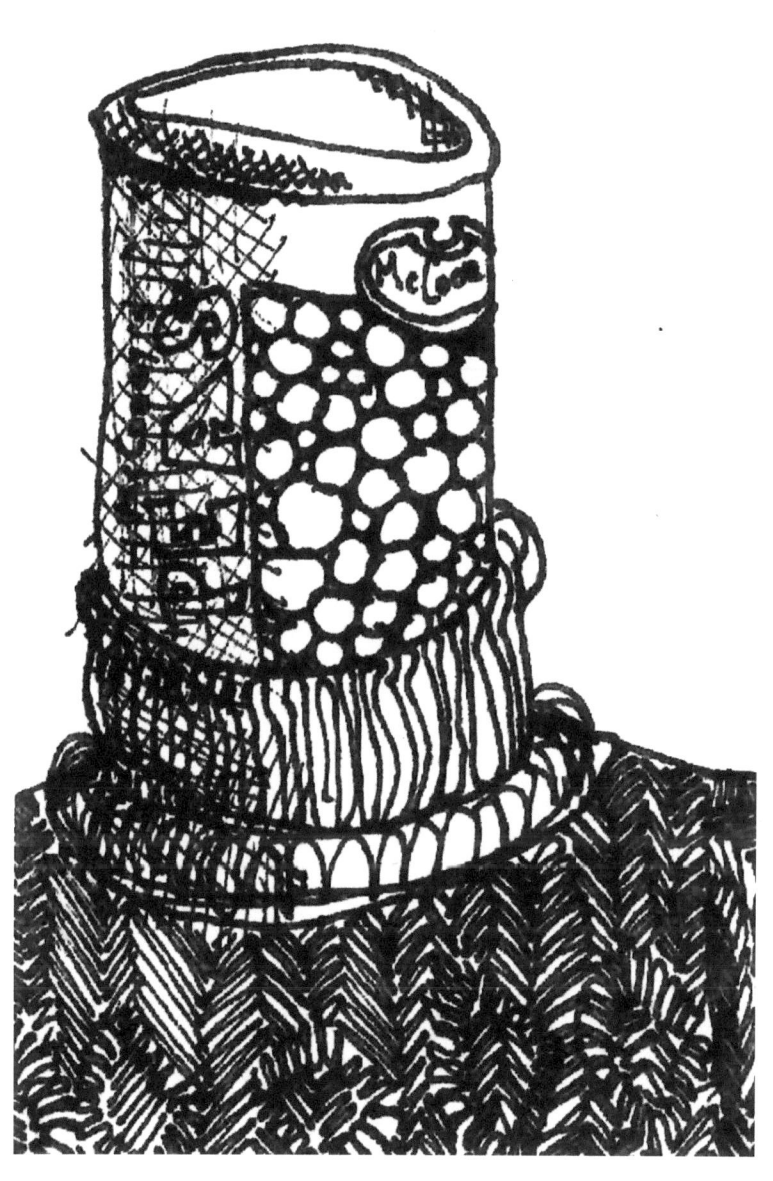

Pea-head

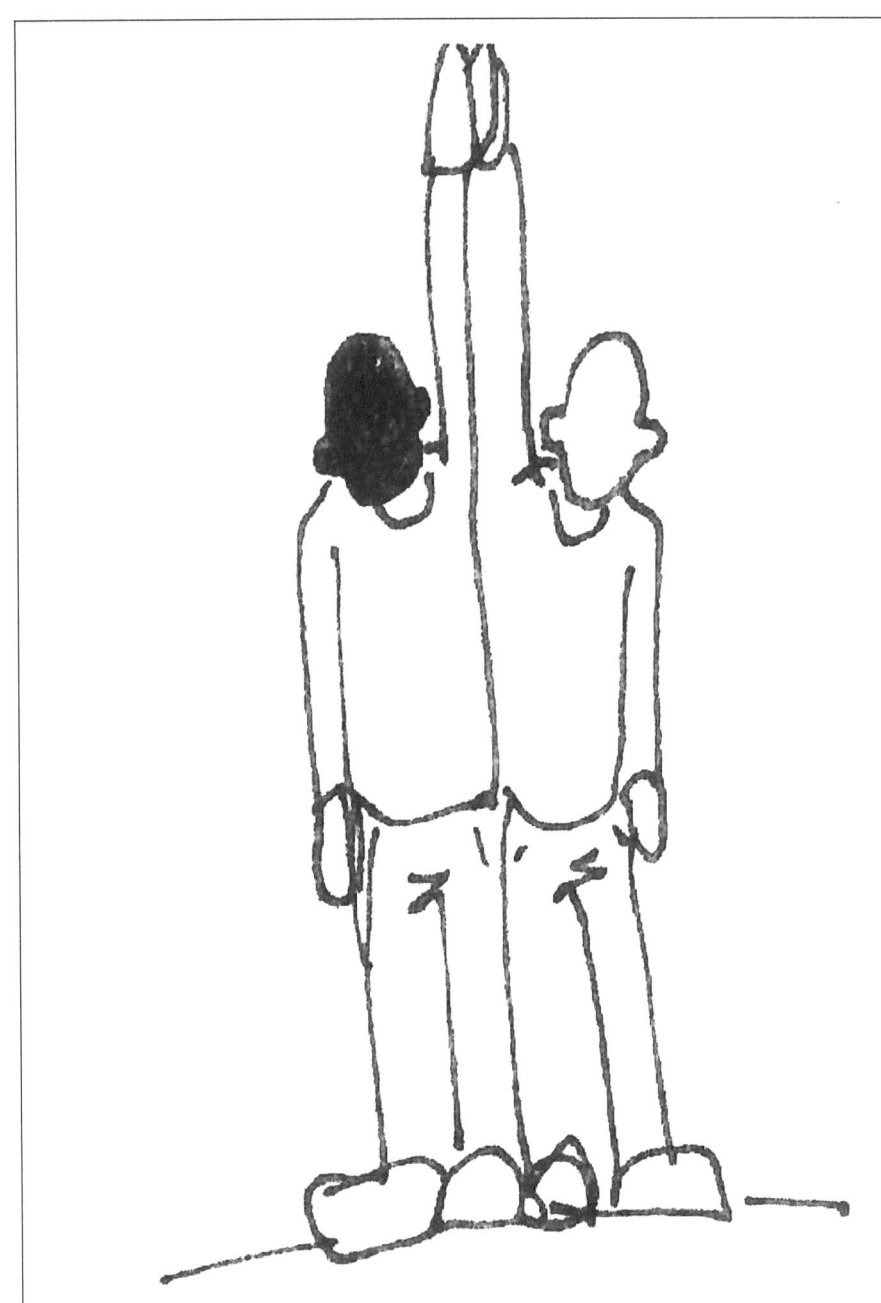

BLACKHEAD/WHITEHEAD

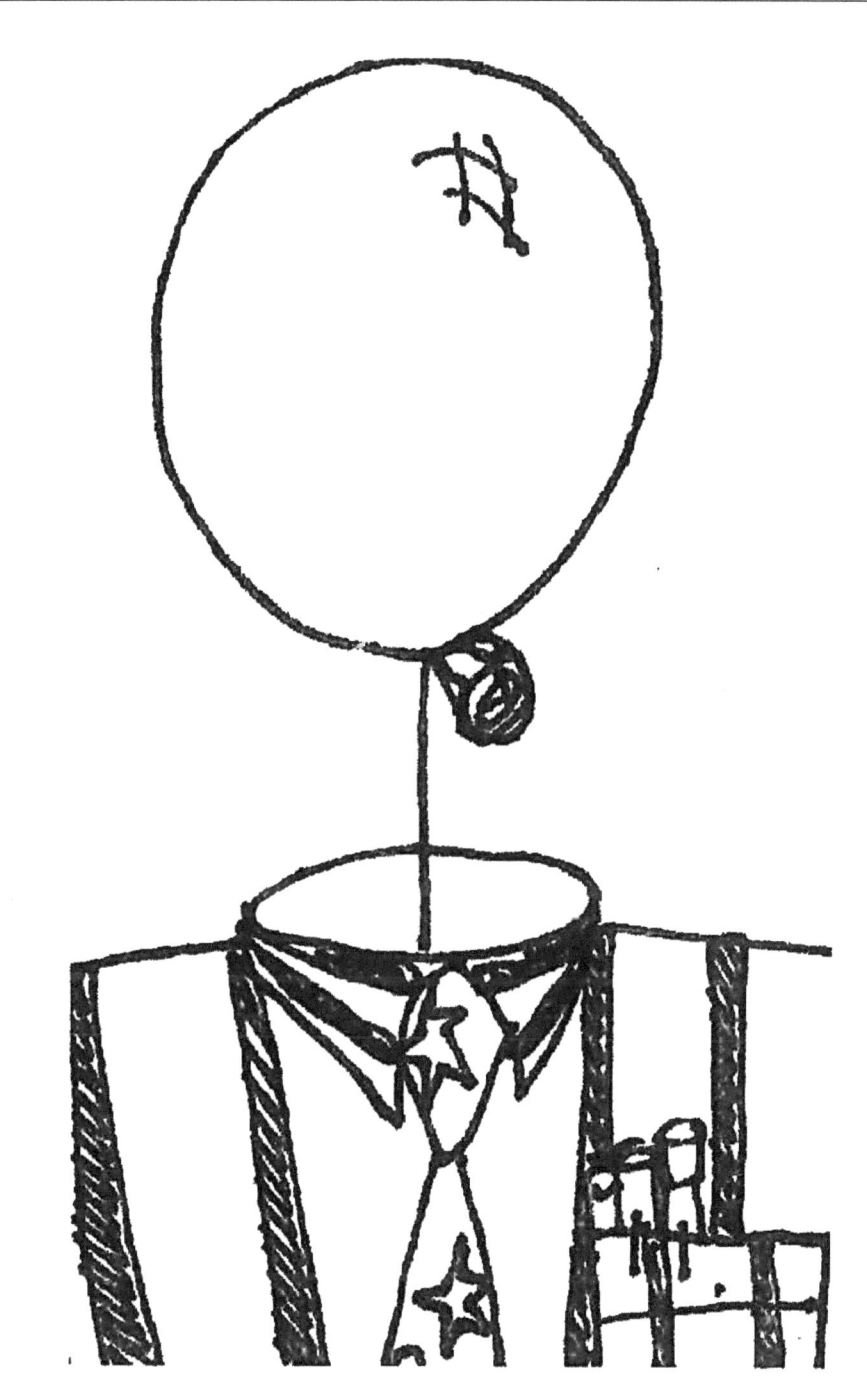

Airhead (number 1)

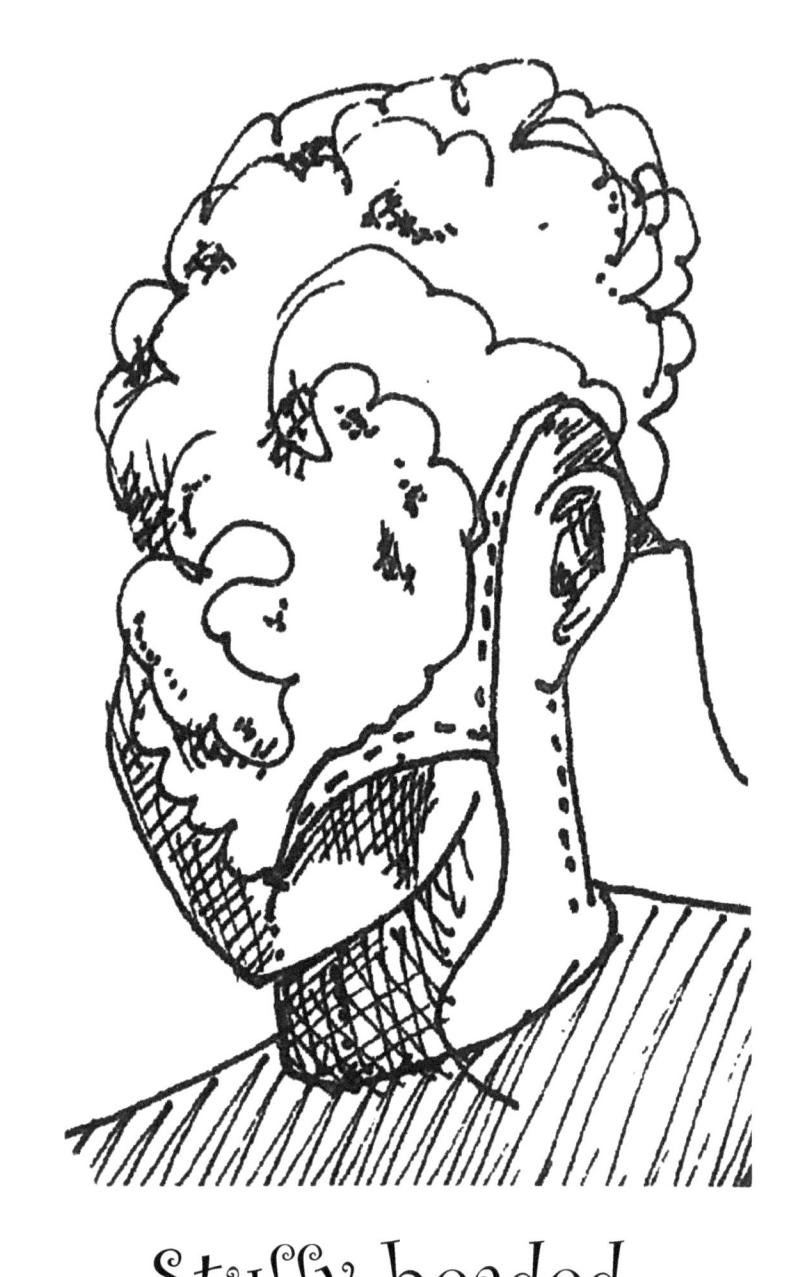

Stuffy-headed

www.ingramcontent.com/pod-product-compliance
Lightning Source LLC
Chambersburg PA
CBHW040247220526
45473CB00001B/401